VOL. V., No. 3

THE JOURNAL
OF
PASTORAL
PRACTICE

JAY E. ADAMS
Editor-in-Chief

Distributed by
BAKER BOOK HOUSE
Grand Rapids, Michigan

ISBN: 0-87552-037-5

PRINTED IN THE UNITED STATES OF AMERICA

CONTENTS

CHRISTIAN WRITING

Because I have spent much time in recent years writing articles and books, it has been necessary to consider what good writing is like. While I am sure that I do not have all of the answers, I think I have a few. In this editorial, in a running outline form, I shall share some of my guiding principles with the hope that some of you will find them useful and be encouraged to put some of your own ideas into print. Christian writing should be

I. Biblical
   —but not academic.
   A. Writing that is informative, scholarly, and substantive,
   B. that uses the original languages and the best commentaries and helps,
   C. need not be dry as dust,
   D. using a stilted, abstract, passive, colorless style
   E. similar to that which is found in most Ph.D. dissertations.

But, instead, it can be,

II. Interesting
   —but not shallow.
   A. Interest can be aroused over a variety of matters:
   B. stories, jokes, unusual experiences.
   C. But, good writing arouses interest from the subject matter itself
   D. by exposing the interest values that are inherent in it,
   E. by relating it significantly to the reader and

1

F. by doing so in a style that at every point is appropriate to him and that grows out of these values.

G. Such a style will have warmth and vividness, will stress active verbs and will adopt the best colloquial form of the day.

Good Christian writing also will be

III. Practical

—but more than a stress on how-to.

A. While how to and good methodology are essential,

B. the writing must address itself to problems and issues

C. and meet needs;

D. in short, it must be motivated by a desire to help someone in some way

E. and should, in fact, do so.

That is why it must be

IV. Substantive

—but clear and simple.

A. It is hard work to strike the proper balance between substance and simplicity,

B. but that is an essential factor.

C. There is a large class of people who need to read substantive material but will do so only if they think that what they are reading isn't.

D. Because most academes refuse to write in a style that will reach them, their scholarship results in too little good.

When necessary, Christian writing must be

V. Polemical

—but not personal.

A. It should attack faulty positions, but not people.

B. However, a writer should never smash a window unless he has another, better one to replace it; negative writing, calculated only to tear down or root up, is a blight.

C. The Christian writer, therefore, must also plant and build.

D. But there must be a zeal for truth, coupled with boldness; people are tired of pussyfooting.

And, finally, conservative Christian writing should be

VI. Innovative
    —but for a purpose.
    A. It must never contain innovation for its own sake.
    B. Rather, innovation must be used to clarify, freshen and strengthen old truths,
    C. and it is important to realize that in many things the most radically innovative step of all is to be more biblical.—J.E.A.

Special Feature

Should Women Teach?

CECIL WILLIAMSON*

There was an organized fellowhip of mature Christian women in the early church who ministered to younger women in the local congregation. If then, why not today? And if today, how? Based on Titus 2:3-5 and related passages, this article seeks to give direction to churches on how to develop and implement such ministries today.

The contemporary church has failed to utilize adequately the gifts for ministry that the Holy Spirit has given to godly women. Far too often we have looked upon women as inferior workers who are to be relegated to menial tasks in the kingdom.

The substance of this material has been implemented in our local assembly. Most women in our cultural setting do not work outside the home. In the opposite cultural setting more account needs to be taken of women as working professionals.

I. *Some Biblical Reasons for Women Teaching in the Local Congregation*

A. That the Word of God Be Not Blasphemed (Titus 2:5)

The Holy Spirit is zealous that the name and word of God be not blasphemed (Titus 2:5). In the Law (Exod. 20:7; Lev. 19:12), in the Prophets (Isa. 52:5; Ezek. 36:20), and in the Epistles (Rom. 2:24; I Tim. 6:1), the Holy Spirit remains steadfast that the name and word of God be not blasphemed.

To maintain that sacred objective He instructs Titus to speak the things that become sound doctrine that those things might be practiced in the lives of the different groups in the Cretan churches (Titus 2:1-10). "But" (Titus 2:1) is a word of contrast which sets Titus in opposition to the false teachers on Crete (Titus 1:10-16) who are subverting entire households by teaching for sordid gain "things they ought not" (Titus 1:11). "You" (Titus 2:1) is emphatic, which heightens the contrast between Titus and the false teachers. Whereas they speak untrue doctrines, he is to continue speaking those things which become sound or healthy doctrine. Among those things becoming

---

* Box 803, Selma, Alabama 36701

healthy doctrine are the directions given to older women about their lives and ministries in Titus 2:3-5. The holy purpose, "that the word of God not be blasphemed" (Titus 2:5), is connected to all that precedes it.[1] If sound doctrine is not spoken and practiced, the word of God will be blasphemed.

By "the word of God" (Titus 2:5) is meant the Christian gospel.[2] This continuing purpose of the Spirit that the word of God not be evil spoken of is similar to Isaiah 52:5, where "name" rather than "word" is used. The apostle quotes the prophet (Rom. 2:24; cf. Isa. 52:5), indicating that the name of God has been blasphemed among the Gentiles because of the ungodliness in the lives of those Jews who professed to believe in and live according to the law. I Timothy 6:1 links "the name" and "the teaching" as the object of possible blasphemy. In Titus 2:5 the substitution of "word" for the more usual "name" gives the phrase added significance.

Contravention of these Christian qualities and duties of Titus 2:3-5 would be a denial of the word of the gospel which they professed to believe.[3] Such denial would cause the Christian gospel to be blasphemed, spoken of reproachfully, reviled, or railed at (Titus 2:5; I Tim. 6:1; James 2:7; Jude 10).

Is the Titus 2:3-5 passage applicable only to a particular cultural situation existing in first-century Crete and thus irrelevant for the church today? The present tendency to explain away certain Pauline writings about women (I Cor. 11:2-16; 14:33-36; I Tim. 2:8-15) as culturally limited or due to Paul's rabbinic background and thus not relevant to the church today causes us to examine Titus 2:3-5 in that context. According to Titus 1:10, 16, there were rebellious men who were to be silenced because they were disturbing entire households. They professed to know God, but by their deeds they denied Him. In this situation in the church and in a culture of which one of the Cretan prophets had said, "Cretans are always liars, evil beasts, lazy gluttons" (Titus 1:12), the apostle is anxious that older Christian women "not make a shipwreck of modesty, sobriety, gravity, and all of the other graces of sex and age."[4] The two prohibitions, "not false accusers" and "not given to much wine" (Titus 2:3), give insight into the contemporary Cretan environment.

---

1. D. E. Hiebert, *The Epistle to Titus* (Chicago: Moody Press, 1957), p. 51.

2. William Hendriksen, *Exposition of the Pastoral Epistles* (Grand Rapids: Baker Book House, 1957), p. 366.

3. John Calvin, *Commentary on the Epistle to Titus,* trans. William Pringle (Edinburgh: T. Constable, 1856), p. 313 (hereafter, Calvin, *Titus*).

4. Thomas Taylor, *An Exposition of Titus* (Grand Rapids: Christian Classics, 1976), p. 146.

When compared to other Pauline passages concerning women and their ministries (Rom. 16; I Tim. 5), Titus 2:3-5 is obviously not an inclusive handbook on the ministry of women. Their ministries in the church surely are not limited to the domestic areas of Titus 2:3-5. Certainly there is a need for training in those areas today. The Holy Spirit has not given us the Titus passage to be used to implement a limited ministry for and to women in these areas; however, the passage does contain valid principles for use in the church today (Titus 2:3-5).

One of these principles is that the word of God will be blasphemed if that word is not spoken and practiced. As the church knows what sound doctrine is in the area of the ministries of women and as that healthy doctrine is spoken and practiced, the word of God will be honored and not blasphemed.

B. That the Body Be Built Up in Love (Eph. 4:16)

Ephesians 4:13 concisely describes the goal of the church in three equivalent ways: unity of the faith and of the knowledge of the Son of God, a mature man, and the measure of the stature which belongs to the fulness of Christ. The verb *katantao*, rendered "attain," is often used of arriving at a destination (Acts 16:1; 18:19; 20:15; 21:7).

The church's destination is initially said to be "the unity of the faith and of the knowledge of the Son of God." The object of both the faith and the knowledge is the Son of God. Charles Hodge reminds us that the faith and the knowledge express or comprehend all the elements of the state of mind objectified in the Son of God, God manifested in the flesh who loved us and gave Himself for us, who died on Calvary and is now enthroned in heaven.[5]

Another description of journey's end for the church is a "mature man." *Teleios* has the connotation of full development (I Cor. 2:6; 14:20; Heb. 5:14). When the church stands complete in glory, it will have reached its goal.

Finally, the church is to arrive at "the measure of the stature which belongs to the fulness of Christ." The standard of perfection for the church is complete conformity to Jesus Christ.

How does the church grow toward perfection? From Christ its Head "the whole body, being fitted and held together by that which every joint supplies, according to the proper working of each individual part, causes the growth of the body for the building up of itself in love" (Eph. 4:16). This journey toward perfection may be visualized.

---

5. Charles Hodge, *Commentary on the Epistle to the Ephesians* (Grand Rapids: Eerdmans Publishing Co, N/A), p. 232.

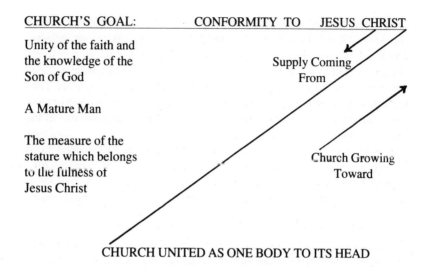

CHURCH'S GOAL: CONFORMITY TO   JESUS CHRIST

Unity of the faith and
the knowledge of the
Son of God

Supply Coming
From

A Mature Man

The measure of the
stature which belongs
to the fulness of
Jesus Christ

Church Growing
Toward

CHURCH UNITED AS ONE BODY TO ITS HEAD

United as one body to its Head, the church, by the supply flowing from Christ through its joints and distributed to every member, grows toward perfection. Calvin comments that it is by love the church is edified. This love manifests itself in the desire of the members for the growth of the other members and the body as a whole.[6]

Christ has distributed gifts to every member of the body (Rom. 12:6; I Cor. 12:7; Eph. 4:7; I Pet. 4:10). As evidenced from the passages containing these verses, gifts determine ministries and are to be used for serving others and building up the body in love.

The instruction of Titus 2:4 is evidence that godly older women have been gifted for these ministries derived from Titus 2:3-5 and related passages. As the older women exercise in love their gifts in ministries to younger women, the local church will be edified and move forward toward the ultimate destination of conformity to Jesus Christ. These ministries should be implemented in the local church so that it will be built up in love.

C. That to Him Be the Glory Forever (Rom. 11:36)

Our chief end is to glorify God and to enjoy Him forever (I Cor. 10:31; Rom. 11:36). The wisdom of God shown in the plan of redemption is unsearchable (Rom. 11:33). To that fact that He is all in all we can but utter the short doxology, "To Him be the glory forever. Amen" (Rom. 11:36).

6. Calvin, *Titus*, p. 314.

It is right that our being should be directed to His glory. "How absurd it would be that the creatures, whom He has formed and sustains, should have any other purpose than to show forth His glory!"[7]

The only rule to direct us how to glorify and enjoy God is His Word. "To discover the Holy Spirit's *telos* is the reason for our exegetical work. . . . we are concerned about discovering the purpose for which the passage was given by the Holy Spirit so that we may use it for the proper purpose for which it was intended. . . ."[8] This profound commitment of faithfulness to God's Word expressed by Dr. Jay Adams becomes necessary as we seek to obey the revealed will of God in the contemporary struggle over the role, function, and ministry of women in the church.

The ultimate purpose of the Holy Spirit in giving us God's will is to direct us how we may glorify and enjoy God. The duty which God requires of us is obedience to that revealed will.

What is obedience to His will in the area of the ministries of women in the church? He gives us a considerable body of instruction which is explored in the following parts of this article. Obedience to that instruction will glorify God (Rom. 11:36).

II. *Identifying from Scripture Those Involved in These Ministries*

A. The Older Women (Titus 2:3)

The feminine noun *presbutidas* is used only here in the Greek New Testament; however, forms of its masculine counterpart are used in Philemon 9, Titus 2:2, and Luke 1:18. In Philemon 9 the apostle speaks of himself as an old man. Just how old he was at the time we do not know. We are aware that at the death of Stephen he was a younger man (Acts 7:58).

Zacharias describes himself to the angel as an old man (Luke 1:18). Although there is disagreement whether the fifty-year-old limitation applied to priests as well as Levites, Jacobus notes that "Zacharias could not have been over fifty years of age, as the duties of the priest's office could not be performed beyond that age."[9]

In a passage (I Tim. 5:2-16) that some consider parallel to Titus 2:3-5, the enrolled widows were not to be less than sixty years of age (I Tim. 5:9). The age limitation of I Timothy 5:9 is necessary because of the complications

---

7. Ibid.

8. Jay E. Adams, *Pulpit Speech* (Phillipsburg, N.J.: Presbyterian and Reformed Publishing Co., 1976), p. 12.

9. Melanchthon Jacobus, *Gospel According to Luke* (New York: N/A, 1856), p. 10.

11

that would arise in having younger widows enrolled. The apostle teaches that when the younger widows "feel sensual desires in disregard of Christ, they want to get married, thus incurring condemnation, because they have set aside their previous pledge. And at the same time they also learn to be idle, as they go from house to house; and not merely idle, but also gossips and busybodies, talking about things not proper to mention" (I Tim. 5:11-13). This explains the necessity of the 60-year minimal age for the enrolled widows; however, it is not possible from Scripture to say definitively that a woman may be designated as "older" when she reaches a certain age. Applying an age definition for the "older women" of Titus 2:3 would be arbitrary at best and at worst not supported by Scripture.

The method used to identify the older women in a local congregation is based on spiritual maturity. It is beneficial to remember that the Old Testament *zaqen* originally "meant one who wears a beard, a mature man," then, "an older man" (Judges 19:16).[10] Those who manifest the Christian virtues given in Titus 2:3 must be viewed as the mature women in the local congregation.

In identifying the mature women in our congregation we sought those who manifested these characteristics. As a part of that which becomes the healthy doctrine of Titus 2:1, Paul instructed Titus to teach the older men in the church to be temperate, dignified, sensible, sound in faith, in love, in perseverance (Titus 2:2). The adverb "likewise" in Titus 2:3 indicates that there is a similarity of requirements for older women and older men. That similarity is for the purpose of befitting sound doctrine.

Older women "are to be reverent in their behavior, not malicious gossips, nor enslaved to much wine, teaching what is good" (Titus 2:3). To be reverent in behavior indicates that in all of life these mature women should manifest a deportment which is becoming to those who have a sacred trust.

"Not malicious gossips" means that they are not slanderers (I Tim. 3:11; II Tim. 3:3). The devil is a slanderer, the father of lies and the accuser of the brethren. Those who belong to Christ are to manifest the opposite conduct and not be false accusers.

"Not enslaved to wine" signifies that mature women do not abuse the usage of wine. They are to be noted for sobriety. They are not to linger beside their wine.

"Teaching what is good" indicates that they are to teach what is according to the word of God. They are to teach that which is good in itself and which will do good in the lives of the ones who are taught.

10. Koehler-Baumgartner, *Lexicon* (Leiden: Brill, 1953), p. 264.

Those women in the local congregation who have the qualities described in Titus 2:3 are to be viewed as the older women and thus qualified for these ministries.

B. The Younger Women (Titus 2:4)

Are the *neas* of Titus 2:4 only young married women with children, or do they also include young married women with no children and young unmarried women? Does consistency require that "the young women" also be selected on the basis of spiritual maturity? These are important questions because the answers determine who will be involved in these ministries.

Because there is no other instance in the Greek New Testament of *neas* being applied in a positive sense to a young person, the word itself does not answer the questions; however, the concept of "new" related to the virtues which follow leads N. J. D. White to remark that "there is possibly a certain fitness in the word applied here to recently married women whom the apostle has perhaps exclusively in view."[11] Charles Eerdman comments that the teaching is "to be given particularly to the younger married women,"[12] and Robert Falconer is more definite in saying that "unmarried women, young widows and children are not in mind. The virtues of worthy wives follow."[13]

However, it does not appear that the restriction to young married women could be substantiated from Titus 2 and related passages. Had the apostle intended to limit the objects of this training to young married women, would he not have used the more common *gunē* in its plural form for "wives"? To argue consistently that *neas* means "new" in the sense of newly married or that "husband-lovers" of Titus 2:4 limits this to young married women, one would have also to make this teaching available only to young married women with children on the basis of "children-lovers" in Titus 2:4. This would reduce unfortunately the number of those getting the benefit of the teaching of the older women to a relatively small proportion of the local assembly. Newly marrieds certainly are included in the *neas;* however, they are not the only recipients of these ministries.

This passage must be considered in the light of others. The apostle writes here as he does elsewhere with the view that marriage is the norm (Eph. 5:22-31; I Cor. 7; Col. 3:18-19). Some may have the gift of celibacy and some may make themselves eunuchs for the sake of the kingdom (Matt.

---

11. *The Expositors Greek Testament*, ed. W. Roberston Nicoll, vol. II, *The Epistle to Titus* (New York: George Doran Co., 1974), p. 192.

12. Charles R. Eerdman, *The Pastoral Epistles of Paul* (Philadelphia: Westminster Press, 1923), p. 148.

13. Robert Falconer, *The Pastoral Epistles* (Oxford: The Clarendon Press, 1937), p. 109.

19:12), but the norm established by God is the permanent covenant of marriage of one man and one woman, who become one flesh (Gen. 2:24; Matt. 19:5; Mark 10:7).

God instituted marriage as the norm through His expressed statement that "it is not good for man to be alone" and through His creation ordinance (Gen. 2:18). It is against this background that Titus 2:3-5 is properly understood. The apostle speaks of women loving their husbands and loving their children because that is his expectation for them. He expects that young women without the gift of celibacy will marry and bear children. That is his specific instruction to young widows (1 Tim. 5:14).

Neither the overwhelming evidence of Scripture as it concerns marriage nor an understanding of the biblical concept of ministry will permit the training of Titus 2:4-5 to be limited to young married women or to young married women with children. Because of the body figure and the commands to mutual ministry within the church, it is inconceivable that such an important segment of the local body, older women, should be limited in their ministries to a proportionately small segment of the church.

Neas may be taken in a more general sense because of the parallel *neoteros* of Titus 2:6. In Titus 2:6 there is no indication that the young men are married or not married. The whole class is encompassed by the word.

C. Two Contrasting Classes (Titus 2:3-5)

The principles derived from Titus 2:3-5 reveal that there are two contrasting groups of women in view here who are designated "older" and "younger." The selection of the older women is based primarily on spiritual maturity. Those who have the qualities described in Titus 2:3 are to be viewed as the "older" or "more mature" women.

In order to begin the program we arbitrarily selected from our local assembly 15 older women and 45 younger women; however, the principles of this ministry are applicable to any number of women.

III. *The Eunice Fellowship*

A. What It Is

A principle derived from Titus 2:3-5 is that though the older women do not occupy an office they are at least an organized fellowship. Membership in this fellowship was limited to those exhibiting the qualities of Titus 2:3. Although these Christian traits should be evident in the lives of all believers in Jesus Christ, evidently they are not.*

---

* Editor's Note: Here is an interesting implication of the idea of interpreting "older" as

14

Is this concept of an organized ministry by women foreign to Pauline thought? This is a crucial point as far as this entire ministry is concerned. In view of I Timothy 5:2-16 an organized ministry by women cannot be said to be foreign to the apostle's teaching. There was to be an enrollment of qualified widows supported by the church who would engage in ministries of prayer and mercy. Specifically, the enrolled widows have qualifications which relate partly to honor and partly to labor. Calvin says, "Accordingly, that they may be better prepared for the discharge of their office, he wishes them to have had long practice and experience in all the duties which belong to it; such as labor and diligence in bringing up children, hospitality, ministering to the poor, and other charitable works."[14]

There was a mutual obligation between the church and the enrolled widows. The church would relieve their poverty. On their part, the widows would minister in areas including child-care, hospitality, humble service toward fellow-believers, and general benevolence.

A difference in the qualifications of those involved in the ministries of I Timothy 5 and Titus 2 emerges. The restriction to widows over 60 years of age in I Timothy 5 is not apparent in Titus 2. What emerges from I Timothy 5 and Titus 2, then, is evidence that within the early church there were organized fellowships of women who ministered.

The admonition in Titus 2:3 that the older women be "reverent in demeanor" tends to support the concept of sacred duties. The word "demeanor" denotes the external deportment as manifesting the inner life. "Reverence" becomes a woman consecrated to God. It is the adjective *hieroprepēs* (*hieros*, sacred, *prepō*, to be fitting, conspicuous, to stand out, to be eminent) which gives some indication that these particular older women were not women advanced in age. These were terms applied to those engaged in sacred service and were befitting to those engaged in a sacred profession (Luke 1:5; Matt. 8:4; 12:4-5). Robert Falconer says that by using these words the apostle is instructing this particular group of women to act as those who have a sacred ministry in the church.[15]

The meaning here is "becoming those who are engaged in sacred service. This is the more striking if, as there is reason to believe, the *presbutidas*

"mature." The two groups are divided not by chronological age (older/younger), but by spiritual condition (mature/less mature). In both categories, presumably, there were younger and older women.

14. John Calvin, *Commentary on the First Epistle to Timothy,* trans. William Pringle (Edinburgh: T. Constable, 1856), p. 129.

15. Falconer, *The Pastoral Epistles,* p. 108.

represented a quasi-official position in the church.''[16] The use of *hieroprepēs* in itself is not sufficient to establish that the older women of Titus 2:3 occupied an office in the church.

The crucial question is whether or not there were organized fellowships of women or women who occupied official or quasi-official positions in the early church. Bishop Lightfoot is emphatic in declaring that deaconesses did comprise an order in the New Testament times. He says that ''the Apostolic Church had its organized ministries of women—its order of deaconesses and its order of widows. . . . As I read my New Testament, the female diaconate is as definite an institution in the Apostolic Church as the male diaconate. Phoebe is as much a deacon as Stephen or Philip is a deacon.''[17]

Church historian Philip Schaff notes that ''the office of deaconess, which under the strict separation of the sexes in ancient times, and especially in Greece, was necessary, and which originated in the apostolic age, continued in the Eastern church down to the twelfth century.''[18] In the Western church, the office of deaconess was abolished by the Synod of Orleans in 533.[19]

It is not within the scope of this article to determine whether or not there should be the office of deaconess in the church today. It is sufficient to note the overwhelming evidence that an official fellowship, quasi-office holders, perhaps even deaconesses, ministered in the early church.

Schaff identifies three groups who filled the office of deaconess. He writes that ''it [office of deaconess] opened to pious women and virgins, and chiefly to widows, a most suitable field for the regular official exercise of their peculiar gifts of self-denying charity and devotion to the welfare of the church. Through it they could carry the light and comfort of the gospel into the most private and delicate relations of domestic life without at all over-stepping their natural sphere.''[20]

Pious women, virgins, and chiefly widows were the deaconesses as that office developed in the early church. Widows were originally considered a special order in the early church and held in high regard because of what is

---

16. Marvin Vincent, *Word Studies in the New Testament* (Grand Rapids: Eerdmans Publishing Co., 1957), p. 341. [That there were unordained, quasi-offical persons is clear from Paul's use of the term ''co-workers.'' In German the position is acknowledged as such and labeled ''mitarbeiter.''—ed.]

17. Charles Ryrie, *The Role of Women in the Church* (Chicago: Moody Press, 1970), p. 85.

18. Philip Schaff, *History of the Christian Church*, vol. III, Nicene and Post-Nicene Christianity A.D. 311–600 (1882; reprint Grand Rapids: Eerdmans Publishing Co., 1979), p. 259.

19. Ibid., p. 261.

20. Philip Schaff, *History of the Christian Church*, vol. I, Apostolic Christianity A.D. 1–100 (1882 reprint Grand Rapids: Eerdmans Publishing Co., 1979), p. 500.

said in I Timothy 5. In the early second century Ignatius wrote to Polycarp, "I salute the households of my brethren with their wives and children, and the virgins who are called widows." Lightfoot interprets the virgins to be the widows who are pure in heart and spirit.[21]

In Ignatius' time there was a recognized order of widows who were really widows and not virgins. About 115 Polycarp, bishop of Smyrna, wrote to the Philippians that the widows were the "altars of God" who must be sober-minded, making intercession without ceasing for all men.[22]

Around 100 Polycarp admonished virgins to make their vows known only to a bishop. By 200 Tertullian was striving to maintain the private character of dedicating one's life to virginity. Around 250 Cyprian admonished older virgins to teach the younger ones. "He treated virgins with more deference than Tertullian did, as if to imply that they had become a recognized order in the church."[23]

From the second century onward, unmarried women were admitted to the order of the widows. For them as well as the widows engaged in charitable works the title of "deaconess" was used.[24] *The Apostolic Constitutions,* written about the middle of the second century, made a careful distinction among the several classes of female workers in the churches—deaconesses, widows, and virgins.[25] It appears that by the end of the second century all of these classes were being referred to as deaconesses. From the third and fourth centuries onwards, numerous texts witness to the existence of deaconesses, at least in the Eastern half of the church. They visited the poor, gave instruction to women, and assisted at the baptism.[26]

McClintock and Strong cite evidence from the church fathers of the existence of the deaconesses in the early church. They state that "Origen (253) speaks of the ministry of women in the church as both existing and necessary. In the western churches the notices are fuller and even more clear. Tertullian (220) speaks of them often. . . . in the fourth and fifth centuries all the leading Eastern fathers refer to deaconesses; e.g. Basil

21. Charles Ryrie, *The Role of Women in the Church* (Chicago: Moody Press, 1970), p. 99.

22. Ibid., p. 100.

23. Ibid., p. 123.

24. Karl Baus, *Handbook of Church History,* vol. I, From the Apostolic Community to Constantine (New York: Herder and Herder, 1965), p. 312.

25. Peter Y. DeYong, *The Ministry of Mercy for Today* (Grand Rapids: Baker Book House, 1961), p. 239.

26. *The Deaconess: World Council of Churches Study No. 4* (Geneva: World Council of Churches, 1966), p. 12.

(379), Gregory of Nyssa (396), Chrysostom (407), Theodoret (457), Sozomen (cir. 439)."[27]

McClintock and Strong relate Titus 2:3 to the deaconesses in the early church. In the writings of Chrysostom and Tehophylact "the rules given as to the conduct of women in I Timothy 3:11 and Titus 2:3 are applied to deaconesses. . . . the social relation of the sexes in the cities of the empire would make it fitting that the agency of women should be employed largely in the direct personal application of Christian truth (Titus 2:3-4). . . . Even the later organization implies the previous existence of the germs from which it was developed."[28]

Although I cannot state as emphatically as Lightfoot that an order of deaconesses existed in the apostolic church, it seems certain that in the apostolic church there were organized ministries by women. I Timothy 5 and Titus 2 are evidences of this. These were the beginnings—the germs, as McClintock and Strong call them—from which the order of deaconess developed in the early church.

Within the early church there was a fellowship of older women whose lives were characterized by those virtues mentioned in Titus 2:3. These women ministered to the younger women.

The concept of an organized ministry by women in the church is Pauline. Therefore, such a ministry should be implemented in the church today. It is the purpose of this paper to encourage pastors to help involve mature women in ministries to less mature women in the local congregation.

Having a name for this fellowship is helpful in identifying those in the local church involved in these specific ministries. A name for the fellowship is also helpful in announcing meetings for and gathering reports from the members of the fellowship.

The name for this ministry, *The Eunice Fellowship,* was suggested by Dr. Edmund Clowney. A pious woman and mother of Timothy, Eunice was a spiritually mature woman who had begun to teach her son while he was a child (Acts 16:1; II Tim. 1:5; 3:15).

B. What It Does

To determine what the Eunice Fellowship does it is necessary to relate Titus 2:3-5 to other passages that speak of the role, function, and ministry of women in the church. Is Titus 2:3-5 an isolated teaching, or does it have

---

27. John McClintock and James Strong, *Cyclopaedia of Biblical, Theological, and Ecclesiastical Literature,* vol. II, C-D (New York: Harper and Brothers Publishers, 1879), p. 709.
28. Ibid.

emphases in common with other Pauline writings? Numerous Pauline passages mention women and their ministries (Rom. 16:1-6, 12, 13, 15; I Cor. 7:2-3, 25-40; 11:2-16; 16:19; Eph. 5:22-23; Phil. 4:2-3; I Tim. 2:8-15; 5:2-16; II Tim. 1:5). In addition, those passages that refer generally to the ministries of believers are of course applicable to Christian women.

There are at least three emphases in Titus 2:3-5—Christian home and family, personal godliness, and ministry by women—that are common to the apostle's writings.

(1) The area for training and ministry in Titus 2:3-5 is consistent with the recurring Pauline emphasis on a Christian home and family. Young women are to be trained to be lovers of their husbands, lovers of the children, good housekeepers, and submissive to their own husbands.

These precepts in Titus 2:4-5 are consistently Pauline. Subjection and faithfulness of wife to husband is a recurring theme in his letters (Eph. 5:22-23; Col. 3:18; I Cor. 7:1-5; 14:33-36; I Tim. 2:8-10). Proper relationships to children and responsibilities in the home for women are also prominent in Paul's writings (I Tim. 5:10, 14; Eph. 6:1-3; I Tim. 5:13-14).

(2) In the immediate context of Titus 2:3-5 the Christian virtues listed are directly related to the areas mentioned. That is to say that a woman does not truly love her husband unless she is discreet, pure, and good. She is unlikely to love her children or to be an excellent housekeeper unless she manifests the traits of goodness and discretion. Older women are to train the younger women to be sensible, chaste, and good (Titus 2:5).

The necessity for these qualities of godliness appears often in Paul's epistles (I Tim. 2:9-10, 15; 5:2, 10; I Cor. 11:2-6; 7:39-40; Rom. 7:1-3). Godliness which is required of all believers is, of course, required by Christian women (Rom. 6:19-22; I Thess. 4:7; I Cor. 1:30; II Thess. 2:13).

(3) The dominant theme emerging from Titus 2:3-5 is that of older women ministering to younger women. Is this an isolated phenomenon, or is the fact of women doing such work of ministry prominent throughout the Pauline letters? The answer is that the apostle widely acknowledges the reality, the desirability and the validity of the ministry of women.

Notable examples are gathered from Romans 16. He commends Phoebe to the church and gives instruction that she is to be received "in the Lord in a manner worthy of the saints and that you help her in whatever matter she may have need of you; for she herself has also been a helper of many and of myself" (Rom. 16:2). She is identified as a *diakonon*, "deacon, servant, minister" (Rom. 16:1). Interestingly enough, this is a masculine noun. She is further described as a *prostatis,* "protectress," of many, including the apostle.

In Romans 16:3-5 he describes the wife and husband team of Priscilla and Aquila as his "fellow workers in Christ Jesus." Mary is acknowledged to be one who had labored hard in the Lord (Rom. 16:12). The verb *kopos,* used in Romans 16:6, 12, is used elsewhere to describe labor in ministry (I Cor. 15:12).

The present active participle of *kopos* indicates that Tryphena and Tryphosa are at present laboring hard in the Lord (Rom. 16:12). Euodia and Syntyche are acknowledged as two women who have shared the apostle's struggle in the cause of the gospel and as his fellow-workers, whose names are in the book of life (Phil. 4:3). He also greets Nympha at Laodicea, who exercises the ministry of hospitality by having the church meet in her home (Col. 4:15).

Passages mentioned previously concerning husband-wife and mother-child relationships certainly indicate that women also have ministries of support, encouragement, hospitality, prayer, and teaching. It becomes clear that the apostle has given us vast information about the wide-ranging ministries of women. Far from being an isolated passage, Titus 2:3-5 is but a part of the greater and prominent apostolic teaching that demonstrates the importance of the ministry of women. This passage, with its emphases on Christian home and family, personal godliness, and ministry of women, is an integral part of the teaching on these important subjects.

Titus 2:3-5 and related passages teach us what the Eunice Fellowship is to do. The sense of *sophronizosin* is that the older women are to bring the younger women to a sound mind and practice (Titus 2:4). The word is from *sōzō,* to save, and *nous,* mind, and is a cognate of the adjective rendered "sensible" in Titus 2:5.

Related concepts derived from *sophronizosin* are to train, teach, school, guide, encourage, instruct, and counsel. For example, "the word, though originally signifying 'to make discreet' or 'prudent,' often came to be used in the more general sense of schooling or admonishing, with a view to the possession of certain things; and the reason, probably, why the apostle here used it, instead of some word expressive simply of teaching or instruction, was that, on account of the youth of the parties in question, he contemplated the necessity of a kind of authoritative disciplinary relationship between older and younger Christian females."[29]

---

29. Patrick Fairburn, *The Pastoral Epistles* (Edinburgh, T. & T. Clark, 1874), p. 273.

Robert Falconer states that the word "is equivalent to *noutheteo*, that they may school them."[30] John Calvin comments that the apostle "shows that it is not enough if their own life be decent, if they do not also train the young women by their instruction to a decent and chaste life."[31]

The ministries of the Eunice Fellowship are derived from *sophronizosin* and its related concepts and other passages which give direction to women's ministries.

C. What Forms the Ministries May Take

Concepts derived from *sophronizosin* give direction to the forms used in implementing these ministries in the local assembly. Among the more interesting observations about the word is that expressed by Falconer that "it is equivalent to *noutheteō*." It is also rendered "to admonish, warn, exhort." The apostle widely uses forms of the verb which are translated "admonish" (Acts 20:31; Rom. 15:14; I Cor. 4:14; I Thess. 5;14; II Thess. 3:15). From this and related principles, Jay Adams has developed successfully his biblical system of nouthetic counseling. The practical effect of relating *noutheteo* to *sophronizosin* is that one of the forms of these ministries is counseling.

From the connotations of *sophronizosin* come other forms for the ministries of the Eunice Fellowship. These include teaching, example, influence, fellowship, prayer, hospitality, deeds and service.

Fellow ministers of the Word, if you too are convinced that you need a Eunice Fellowship in your church, then why not begin to develop a program this year? The benefits can be deep and lasting as they have been in my congregation.

30. Falconer, *The Pastoral Epistles*, p. 109.
31. Calvin, *Titus*, p. 314.

Counseling

HOWARD A. EYRICH
Editor

Howard A. Eyrich is a counselor in the CCEF offices in Atlanta and Macon, Georgia. He holds the Th.M. from Dallas Theological Seminary and the D.Min. from Western Conservative Baptist Seminary in Portland, Oregon.

Counsel on Being Reconciled to Our Brother

TIM CRATER

In the pastoral ministry, there are abundant opportunities to counsel with people about problems in their relationships with others. Much of the unhappiness, guilt, and depression experienced by Christians is occasioned by unresolved differences between themselves and others. This is comparable to a physical burden which, if carried throughout the day, makes one less able to carry on his normal functions in life. Unresolved tensions comprise a kind of freight which diminishes the mind's capacity to function in optimal fashion, robbing humans of a good measure of joy and peace. If, as the Lord Jesus insisted, loving other human beings made in God's image is the second most important thing we can do (Matt. 22:39), then it is reasonable to conclude that breakdowns in our relationships with others can be a prime source of trouble in the Christian life. Apprehensions about going places for fear we will see someone whom we have offended, or who has offended us, do not make for a peaceful and contented life, and yet very often people are willing to let such tensions continue without any effort to resolve them.

In the Lord's scheme of interpersonal relalationships there are at least three sources of disruptive trouble between individuals: (1) I may have offended; (2) I may have been offended; (3) there may have been a misunderstanding. In Matthew 5:23-24, the Lord tells us that if you are worshiping and "remember that your brother has something against you, leave your offering there before the altar and go your way; first be reconciled to your brother, and then come and present your offering" (NASB). Relationships have thus a higher priority than religious activity. In Matthew 18:15, He speaks to the time when "your brother sins against you," and of our need to "go and reprove him in private. . . ." In Joshua 22:10-34, we see a prime example of tensions caused by mere misunderstanding, with both parties

25

having commendable motives and objectives, but the one's actions are misinterpreted by the other. The two and a half tribes in Transjordan built an altar and the other tribes of Canaan thought it was for idol-worship. In reality, it was an altar of witness for future generations, so that the sons of the tribes in the land of Canaan could not make the sons of the Transjordanian tribes stop worshiping the Lord in the promised land.

Any one of these three factors, or even some combination of them, may be the cause of tension between people and certainly should be kept in mind when doing pastoral counseling. In each case where there is an offense, the reader is told to take the initiative, whether he offended or was offended. Reconciliation, which restores fellowship between humans, is important enough that wherever one stands with respect to the offense, it is incumbent upon him to "go." While we are not commanded in Joshua to go, it is clear that the tribes which suspected offense on the part of the other tribes took the initiative to investigate, and were prepared to take action if their suspicions were confirmed. It seems clear that pastors and counselors should stand ready to exhort believers in Christ to follow out these instructions in their personal relationships; whatever the circumstance, they should be urged to go. Ideally, two people separated by some matter should meet each other coming for reconciliation. Paul calls the ministry a ministry of reconciliation (II Cor. 5:18-19), to God first and foremost, but also to those made in His image, which includes immediate family, Christian family, and our neighbor wherever he is.

Most of this will not be new material, and it isn't my purpose to cover the basics of reconciliation. I have found, however, that in the frequent attempts made by Christians to reconcile, certain questions arise as to when and how the reconciliation effort should be made. There are certain ramifications of the teaching which are not explicitly addressed in the passages cited above, but which warrant some brief reflection.

Confession of Thoughts

One question which has arisen in this area is whether it is necessary and proper for us to go to others and confess evil thoughts which we may have had against them or for them. I have had Christians acknowledge that they have come to terms with some kind of illicit thoughts or attitudes toward others, and now wonder if they should not go to such persons and confess in an attempt to reconcile with them. There was no question that the thoughts were, for the one thinking them, sin, and that they needed to judge them, seek God's forgiveness and turn from them. Since another person was the object of their thoughts, they wonder if they should not acknowledge to such a person what has been going on in order to clear things up completely.

Such a desire, to clear up the matter completely in order to obtain a clear conscience, surely is commendable. However, it does not seem either necessary or wise from a biblical point of view for us to confess sins which have remained only in our own hearts, even when such thought-sins involve others. When the Lord gave His instruction in Matthew 5:23-24, He indicated that we are to take the initiative in cases where *we* have offended only when we *know* our brother has something against us.[1] This means that in the mind of the brother, at least, something is wrong with the relationship; he has been offended in some manner. In Matthew 5:22, the Lord has prefaced His instructions about reconciliation by speaking of a brother actually saying something offensive ("Raca," "you fool") to his brother, and He undoubtedly, therefore, envisioned the reconciliation process as the proper step for such a brother. But when you say something or do something offensive, then clearly the other person is involved and some sort of bilateral effort must be made if there is to be peace.

But when one merely has evil thoughts, such as lust or hatred, then the other person does not necessarily know of them and is not therefore offended by them. He has no occasion to have something against us and, it would seem, there is thus no rationale for a conciliatory effort on our part. One need not dwell long on this to appreciate why the Lord left no teaching which would urge us to go in such circumstances. If we went to people when we merely had entertained evil thoughts toward them, but which we subsequently conquered, we might end up creating an offense where there wasn't one to begin with. A brother who did not know we had envied him, or a sister who did not know we had lustful thoughts toward her could very easily take offense when he or she heard that we had such thoughts; at the very least it could jeopardize our fellowship with them. A current proverb of note goes something like this: "If it ain't broke, don't fix it." That seems to speak quite well to the issue of reconciliation when the brother has not been offended, when we have merely had evil thoughts which have not issued in any outward manifestation which could offend.

Now this is not to say that sinful thoughts are trivial. Clearly, they must be judged as sin and turned from. Even if our brother doesn't see them, they are

---

1. Of course, in a case where, e.g., one has cheated another (and it is yet unknown to him), the brother should go and straighten out the matter. Transgressions, not thoughts, must be dealt with. Often (almost always in time), thoughts lead to transgressions, e.g., envy leading to abrupt words or avoidance of another.—ed.

offensive to God, disrupt our fellowship with Him, and may ultimately issue in offensive acts if not checked while yet in the thought stage. The point here is that mere thoughts do not offend and therefore do not require us to go and reconcile with the one who was the subject, or object, of the thoughts.

The False Confession

Another problem related to the reconciliation process is the willingness on the part of sincere people to go and ask forgiveness of others when they either don't know what they did to offend or else aren't fully convinced that they did anything wrong. In their eagerness to make peace they assume that it is showing the proper humility and grace to take the initiative and ask forgiveness anyway.

This problem has surfaced frequently in discussions with Christians about their relationships to others and what steps they should take to restore broken ones. As I examined the particular problem with them, their sincerity is usually evident, but they have no precise understanding of what they did to provoke the tension that exists. I have explained on such occasions that it would really not be honest to go to the person and ask forgiveness when in their hearts they were not convinced they did anything wrong, or they are not aware of any particular grievance which the other person could have against them.

What they can and should do in such situations is go to the person with the purpose of *investigating* the nature of the problem. It may turn out that any one of the three factors cited above, or a combination thereof, will surface during the discussion and they will then know how to proceed. If the other person states an offense, and the one going agrees, then he can ask forgiveness sincerely. If the one going doesn't agree, and thinks rather that the fault lies with the other person, he may reprove him, as Matthew 18 instructs us to do. If the two cannot come to a resolution of the problem, then perhaps third party mediation is called for on the order of that suggested in the same passage (see Matt. 18:16; also I Cor. 6:5). It may turn out after all that a misunderstanding has occurred and it can be resolved during this discussion. But whatever the outcome, they ought certainly to avoid the hypocrisy and insincerity involved in a false confession, even if their motives are good.[2]

The Unexamined Charge

The Christian church has people come into it from each extreme of the

2. This situation is more common than may be supposed. False confession must be avoided at all costs, not only to avoid hypocrisy, but because it really fails to deal definitively with the issues(s) involved.—ed.

self-esteem spectrum. It has those who think more highly of themselves than they ought (Rom. 12:3), and it has those who invariably think the worst about themselves (self-abasement). It has always seemed to me that the ministry of the church of Christ was in part to facilitate the work of God in exalting the lowly and humbling the proud (I Pet. 5:5-6; James 4:6). In regard to the reconciliation process, there are plenty around who will not receive anyone's reproof and cannot believe they do or have done anything wrong; they dismiss criticism and reproof out of hand. Such folks may end up in the final stages of church discipline outlined in Matthew 18 before they suspect that perhaps they too have faults.

On the other hand, there are folks in the body of Christ who are willing to believe uncritically any charge against them. Seeing themselves in very lowly terms, they conclude they must have done it, it must be so; after all, *they* know what they are really like inside. It seems evident that our objective in this regard is to teach members of the church to "examine everything carefully" and to "hold fast to that which is good" (I Thess. 5:21, NASB). While in the original context this referred to prophetic utterances in the local assembly, it is also quite good advice for any would-be reproof which represents itself as coming from the Holy Spirit through a Christian. We ought not to presume anything, either our own guiltlessness (we are, after all, sinners), or our own sinfulness (we can also be wronged by others). Instead, we ought to examine the charge as objectively as we can, and if we have sinned, then we can judge it and confess it to God and man and turn from it. If we have not sinned, then the problem lies elsewhere and perhaps needs arbitration by fellow believers (I Cor. 6:5).

Every person has the right to testify about himself, as Paul did in I Corinthians 4:4, that "I am conscious of nothing against myself" (NASB). My objective assessment of myself, in other words, is a valid part of the whole picture. Paul added, "I am not by this acquitted," meaning it isn't the final word on matters, but my self-judgment is to be regarded as a legitimate piece of evidence. If it is wrong, the facts will show it and I'll repent.

We are not into self-abasement any more than we are into pride; what we are about is the truth, the truth about ourselves and the truth about the situation we may find ourselves in with respect to someone else. As Paul puts it in Romans 12:3, we are "to think so as to have sound judgment" (NASB).

Forgiveness and Optional Matters

There have been occasions when an offending party has acknowledged his sin, sought forgiveness of the other party and then insisted that if the offended party has truly forgiven him, a practical matter between them which was placed in jeopardy through the sin will proceed as before. This raises the question of whether if, through sin, one breeches a contract of some sort, releasing the other party from his obligation thereby, does forgiveness require in every case that the original obligation be re-instituted? A marital twist to this question involves the question of whether a mate whose partner commits adultery may truly forgive the offender yet nevertheless proceed with divorce on the basis of Jesus' exception in Matthew 5 and 19.

While there may be some instances in which forgiveness and the optional matter go hand in hand, I believe that they do not necessarily coincide every time. If a developer, let's say, fails to live up to a time and money commitment to investors through a moral failure of some sort, though the investors may genuinely forgive him, it is not incumbent upon them as part of their forgiveness to renew their contract with him if they deem it to be in the best interest of the project to secure another agent. But Christians, in the business world and elsewhere, have sought to use this issue to get another crack at an opportunity they missed through their own default. It seems to me that not only are the offended parties free from obligation from a spiritual standpoint, but that it is a further offense and a dishonorable act for a supposed Christian to try to question the genuineness of the ones offended in order to get back into a lost opportunity. Such an attitude suggests continuing carnality rather than genuine repentance, whereas a truly repentant attitude will concede that nothing further is owed to the penitent. David set the example for this in II Samuel 15:25-26, where he says: "If I find favor in the sight of the LORD, then He will bring me back again, and show me both it [the ark] and His habitation. But if He should say thus, 'I have no delight in you,' behold here I am, let Him do to me as seems good to Him" (NASB).

While every legal consideration should be explored, and every scriptural principle considered case by case, it seems to me that forgiveness, the willingness to restore fellowship, does not necessarily require resumption of original contractual obligations in material matters. Practical considerations may well make it prudent to take other measures and the genuineness or sincerity of forgiveness ought not to be questioned merely because those other measusres were pursued.

Women Reproving Men

Related to the issue of reconciliation is the question of whether it is proper, given the biblical teaching on submission, for women to reprove

30

men, for wives to reprove their husbands for sins against them. Not a few wives have wondered if this option was open to them. I say sin "against them" deliberately here, for modern textual theory has led again to the elimination of another important qualification of the Lord's teaching. The phrase "against you" is eliminated from Matthew 18:15 in most modern versions, while the Majority Text retains this reading. Being an advocate of the latter, I understand the Lord to be teaching that we are to go and reprove where sin is against us, a teaching in concert with Leviticus 19:17-18.

I am persuaded that there is nothing in the Bible which would prohibit a woman from exercising this option. It seems to me that the two passages cited above make no effort to restrict the right of reproof to men only; such teaching seems rather to be directed at the believing community at large. If a woman's brother, whether it be her husband or another Christian man, sins against her, then she appears to have the same right as any Christian man to initiate the proceedings of Matthew 18:15f. For a woman to reprove a man who is sinning against her hardly seems to be of the same order as her refusing to submit to his leadership and authority in the home or church. Certainly, this privilege ought not to become a pretext for nagging her husband, for not submitting to him in legitimate areas, or for acting disrespectfully toward him.

One pertinent Old Testament example is Abigail. I realize there are some who think Abigail stepped out of line in going to David. I do not think so, and believe there are a number of good reasons in the text of I Samuel 25 which establish that she was on solid ground in what she did. While David had not yet sinned against her, her husband, and their household, it is clear that he was on his way to do just that. She perceived what was happening and took action to save lives. In effect, she confronted David *prior to* his sin against her and against Nabal's household so that many lives could be spared. The text has nothing but praise for her, and David himself recognizes that her coming was of God, for he says in verse 32, "Blessed be the LORD God of Israel, who sent you this day to meet me" (NASB). He acknowledges that he was about to sin and take his own revenge, and attributes his repentance to her coming to meet him to confront him about his planned evil.

The attitude in which a woman does this is all-important. It's important with men who go and reprove too, but because of the additional factor of God's created order among men and women, it is especially necessary for a woman to emulate Abigail in the sweetness and gentleness of her approach. Her speech is a paradigm of wisdom and prudence, which David recognizes,

31

and because she approached him with humility and wisdom, she won him over (cf. Matt. 18:15). I personally advise women that they take the initiative here, and spend some time in helping them frame the particular approach they should take when they go to reprove a man. On principle, I see nothing which would prohibit them from engaging in this important process.

The Covered Multitude

When first informed of the teaching on reconciliation, there are some folks in the church who get carried away in their enthusiasm for reproving and make it their intent to reprove on every matter which comes up. I've found it necessary to stress that, while there are clearly some sins for which we will want to reprove others, it is also true that "love covers a multitude of sins" (I Pet. 4:8, NASB). In a marriage and in relationships in general, there are plenty of things which, to a minor degree, offend or bother us about someone else and which, out of love for others, we must simply overlook. Proverbs 19:11b says of a man that "it is his glory to overlook a transgression" (NASB).

This is not to suggest that it is unspiritual for someone to go and reprove rather than to overlook an offense. It is only to say that there are a multitude of interpersonal problems that should simply be covered, overlooked; and the act of reproof should be reserved for those things which we simply cannot get over and which cause continuing problems between ourselves and others. Sometimes in the Christian life it is good to ask ourselves, "Why not rather be wronged?" (I Cor. 6:7). Instead of pursuing reproof immediately, why not ask if the issue warrants this step, if it may perhaps be one which we should simply overlook? If not, then reproof is the legitimate remedy to pursue.

Loving Those Who've Offended

Another problem which has arisen in relation to one's relationship with those who've offended him has to do with love. We are told, "love your enemies, do good to those who hate you . . ." (Luke 6:27, NASB). I have often discussed with troubled Christians the difficulty of doing this, or, rather, the seeming difficulty of doing it. One young Christian was having difficulty loving a certain teacher who, it turned out, was acting in an offensive way toward him. He was disturbed that he could not seem to conjure up the requisite feeling for this teacher that he believed the Lord was commanding him to have for her. Though he had voiced his grievance to her, she continued doing the thing that was offensive to him, and he continued to be offended. She had become his enemy of sorts, and he was making an earnest attempt to love her as his enemy in accordance with what the Lord had taught.

It appears to me that there is a problem here in the way we understand love. The young student had equated the good feelings that have been commonly associated with love in the secular world with the love we are biblically commanded to have, for loved ones as well as enemies. But as I understand biblical love in this regard, it is not so much a feeling to be felt as it is an active policy which we are to pursue in spite of the fact that our feelings for the person may not be good. That is why "doing good to those who hate you" is so closely associated with love in Luke 6. To love one's enemies, or even one's friends, in this sense is to pursue a policy of *acting* in their interest, so that if they hunger we feed them, and if they thirst we give them drink (Rom. 12:20); that is how we love them. We don't *feel* love for them, we *exercise* love toward them.

Actually, what we sense is lacking in a relationship with one who is offensive to us is affection, that warm desire for his fellowship and companionship. Paul spoke to the Thessalonians of his having "thus a fond affection (*homeiromenoi*) for you" (I Thess. 2:8, NASB). That is the normal, natural feeling which is a by-product of fellowship. It cannot be pumped up artificially in the absence of fellowship; it comes only when we are free of offenses between one another. But while affections are feelings, and by-products of fellowship, love is a policy which must be implemented regardless of fellowship and affection, or lack thereof. While we may not have affections and a warm longing for our enemy, and it would be abnormal if we did have such feelings, we may yet *act* in his best interest, *do* him good, and so forth. If we ever resolve the offenses between us, then quite naturally we would expect the affection to begin to grow and ultimately to blossom again as a result of reconciliation. But until there is reconciliation, honest dealing with sin and forgiveness, there will not be—we should not expect there to be—and should not condemn ourselves for not having, feelings of affection toward those who've offended us. That simply is not what God is asking of us. He is asking that we *exercise* love toward them. In my own personal life and in the lives of others, I have found that it is possible to act in the best interest of someone else who is offensive, when I have not found it possible to conjure up a feeling of affection for such people. The sweetness of affection between people, that sin destroys or interrupts, is one of the main incentives for us to rectify broken relationships, as it can only be experienced when offenses are dealt with first, when fellowship is restored.[3]

A Two-Way Street

One final observation with respect to peaceful relationships. Christians have a way of taking all the responsibility on themselves when they should not, and I have personally seen this tendency at work in regard to reconciliation. In Romans 12:18 Paul wrote, "If possible, so far as it depends on you, be at peace with all men" (NASB). Here is the recognition that reconciliation is a two-way street, and a pastor should be concerned to establish that the one who has sought advice has done all that he is scripturally required to do in order to reconcile with another. He should be prepared, however, to assure the one who has tried that he *has* done all and that there appears to be no more he can do from his side. If the other person is unwilling to reconcile, then the burden is on him; the one who tried is free from the II Timothy 3:3 indicates that there is a sin of being "irreconcilable," one which should not be true of Christians, but also one which Christians may encounter in others with whom they are seeking to reconcile. The counselor's task in this case is to help determine just how far it depends on each party and whether the one before him has gone that far or not. Peace is a two-sided matter.

---

3. It is only *after* you have fixed the flat that you can enjoy the ride.—ed.

What Do You Do When Church Discipline Fails?

G. R. FISHER

Editor's Introduction

You have heard an increasing number of calls for the exercise of church discipline. You have also no doubt heard of some incidents of very un-Christian and questionable exercise of church discipline. In the history of the church, when a doctrine has laid dormant, its reaffirmation has brought misuse and misunderstanding. Obviously this has occurred with the practice of church discipline.

It is for this reason that Rev. Fisher's brief but practical article is commended to you. He faces the doctrine squarely. But, he shows us how to use it as a tool—together with the safety gear needed to avoid causing injury—and not as a club, however inadvertently.—H.A.E.

The title is a little misleading. I believe if we do what God expects of us and proceed according to biblical principles, we cannot fail in the eyes of God, even though others fail to respond as we would wish. I guess the question really is, "What do we do when people fail to repent when church discipline is carried out?" In the first few cases in which our church exercised discipline, the hardest thing we had to face was the fact that things didn't clear up and people didn't repent as we had expected. Church discipline is always difficult, pressure-filled, even agonizing, business. Let me offer a few suggestions as we move toward the final step of Matthew 18, where we will, as a church, be making the awesome judgment to count another professing brother or sister "as an heathen and a publican."

1. *Be sure that the situation warrants church discipline.* I have seen people "jumping the gun," rushing to judgment for infractions that could have been handled personally, or, in some cases, even overlooked (Prov. 10:12; James 5:19-20). The New Testament calls on us to exercise love,

forbearance, patience, etc. However, if the sin or sins are *open, flagrant, continuous, public,* and fall into the categories of I Corinthians 5:9-11, Romans 16:17, Titus 3:10-11, or II Thessalonians 3, we are safe in moving ahead in church discipline. Church discipline is for sin in the extreme. Be careful not to misuse the procedure. Move prayerfully and carefully through the Matthew 18 steps one at a time.

2. *Be sure you have a well-thought-out and agreed-upon policy* that people are aware of when they come into membership. Avoid the "we didn't know" or "it was sprung on us" cop-out that will only be used as a smoke screen later. (See Appendix I, "Church Discipline Procedure," for a suggested wording.) Other helpful sources for a study of church discipline and wording can be found in *The Westminster Confession of Faith for Study Classes,* by G. I. Williamson (Presbyterian and Reformed), pages 235-39, and in other church constitutions.

3. *Be sure that every sincere attempt has been made at reconciliation.* Has the first one going gone in the spirit and attitude of Galatians 6:1? Have the few more going gone prayerfully *offering concrete suggestions* on how the sin can be put away and changes made? Has hope and help really been offered, or has there been a judgmental spirit and a "dressing down" of the offender? Has the desire for reconciliation and restoration been communicated effectively?

4. *Be sure to expect reactions if there is no repentance.* Do not be surprised if there are harsh innuendos such as "the pastor doesn't care," "the board is unloving," "those people are harsh Pharisees and know nothing of love and forgiveness." (By this they *mean,* "let me stay in my sin.") The unrepentant will always try to blameshift and cover. They "hide and hurl." But love that does not discipline is not love; it is a wishy-washy sentimentality. True love demands discipline (Heb. 12:6-8). We can't ignore gross sin, and we must seek solutions while correcting the sinner. Unrepentant sinners may even initiate a letter-writing campaign so "the congregation can hear our side," as they put it. Some people are prone to do this. If all this energy and effort were put into reconciliation and repentance, what a fantastic recovery could be made! The letter writing should be seen as a further effort to "sow discord" and avoid the authority of the church leadership. It is a violation of Hebrews 13:17.

Innuendos and threats may grow in intensity. Do not be too upset if the pastor, board, and congregation are threatened with a lawsuit. This threatening has occurred both to me and to other pastor friends when people became adamant in their refusal to change. Expect something radical like this and, if it comes, don't panic. Be ready to "give an answer." (See Appendix II for a sample of a letter used in one situation.) I have never seen a person carry out the threat, although it is possible. If the threat is acted upon, then counsel from a competent Christian attorney is advisable. In my opinion, I Corinthians 6:1 would apply to the offender and not the church. "Before the saints" is what the church is seeking to do.

5. *Be sure you have all the facts in writing.* Jesus said, "judge with righteous judgment" (John 7:24). As soon as you sense you are moving into formal church discipline, records should be made of all meetings, contacts, phone calls, etc. Too much can be forgotten or confused, especially if the offending brother is committed to throwing you off the track. Remember, our God is a "God of order." A written invitation should be sent registered mail (receipt kept) to inform the offender of the final meeting.

6. *Be sure the board is totally agreed on the procedure of discipline and the manner in which the information is brought to the congregation.* The whole process is stressful enough without division on procedure, etc. We have found that a *reading* of all the events leading up to the final action brings perspective to the congregation and keeps the meeting on track. We have found also that *written* testimony from the witnesses helps to take stress from them and make the testimony more objective. Whether all the congregation votes to ratify the recommendation of the board, as in our case, or the elders report the decision to the congregation (as in the case of some congregations), the procedure should be brought to a *definite, final* conclusion with no confusion as to what has been done. In short, be sure the people of the congregation understand fully what the pastor and board *expects them to do* (accept a proposal, ratify a proposal, or whatever) and *keep the discussion on target.* The board and moderator should know exactly where they are going and be clear about it. It is absolutely essential that the board and pastor display a "united front."

In the event the offending party decides to "smoke screen" ("What about what so and so did last year?") in that final meeting, the moderator must insist that they stay with the purpose of the meeting and the facts at hand. He should just keep reading pertinent excerpts from the written report as to what has been done and the objections will soon stop. One fear that a board of sensitive men (and they should be) will have to cope with is the idea stated or felt that they "may split the church." In most cases they may anyhow if they do not act decisively. They may also be concerned that they will lose respect in the eyes of those they lead. It is far better to obey the Lord of the church (discipline is *His* procedure) than to fear man. In the *long run,* it will be better for the church if God weeds out those sympathetic with sin. And, it is always true, properly exercised discipline ultimately leads to respect.

I know of a church that let sin go by and never dealt with a serious problem in an elder's life. Twelve years later that man almost destroyed the church after he gained influence. It could have been much easier to deal with him earlier.

7. *Be sure that once the church has acted, i.e., voted to excommunicate, letters are sent to those who are excommunicated,* telling them they have no voice or vote and expressing to them the continued hope that there will be repentance and restoration. The letters should be *registered* and receipts kept. Copies of those should be put in the church files as permanent records.

To do things God's way is to be a success regardless of the way others respond. We must remember that the objectives of church discipline are to honor God, to win the offender, to restrain evil in the congregation, and to remove it by excommunication if necessary. It protects the right and cherishes the good. It keeps sin from being accepted. Our approach must be balanced and biblical. The end result (whether through repentance or not) is to glorify God through our obedience. Our hope and comfort during all of its stressful stages is found in the words of Jesus: "And I also say to you . . . whatever you shall bind upon earth shall have been bound in heaven . . ." (Matt. 16:18-19, NASB).

Rev. G. R. Fisher
P.O. Box 514
Bricktown, N.J. 08723

APPENDIX I

CHURCH DISCIPLINE

Formal church discipline will be carried out by the deacons (elders) and pastor in keeping with the steps of Matthew 18:15-18: "And if thy brother sin against thee, go, shew him his fault between him and thee alone; if he hear thee, thou has gained the brother. But, if he hear thee not, take with thee one or two more, that at the mouth of two or three witnesses every word may be established. And if he refuse to hear them, tell it to the church; and if he refuses to hear the church also, let him be unto you as a gentile and a publican. Verily I say unto you: what things you loose on earth shall be loosed in heaven."

It is assumed that any first step of any individual to another would be carried out in the spirit of Galatians 6:1: "Brethren, if any man be overtaken in any

38

trespass, ye which are spiritual, restore such an one in a spirit of meekness; looking to thyself lest thou also be tempted.''

When formal discipline has been initiated at the board level, no members will be allowed to resign. That is, no withdrawal by letter will be accepted by the congregation.[1] Discipline would be dictated in the event of gross, open and continued sin or in a blatant disregard of one's church covenant. At every level, church disciplining is to be seen as being restorative (that is, with the hope of repentance and restoration of those dealt with), not punitive (looked on as a punishment).

If formal discipline must be carried out by the congregation to the dismissing from membership of a member or members, until there is demonstrated repentance and change, the congregation is to follow through with the following scriptural injunctions in regard to those individuals, except in cases where a husband or wife or children must remain in the same home. Romans 16:17: ''Now I beseech you, brethren, mark them which are causing the divisions and occasions of stumbling, contrary to the doctrine which ye learned, and turn away from them.'' I Corinthians 5:11-13: ''But now I write to you not to keep company, if any man that is named a brother be a fornicator, or covetous, or an idolater, or a reviler, or a drunkard, or an extortioner; with *such an one not to eat*. For what do I have to do with those that are without? Do not ye judge them that are within, whereas God judgeth them that are without. *Put away that wicked man from among yourselves.*''

II Thessalonians 3:6, 14: ''Now we command you, brethren, in the name of our Lord Jesus Christ, That ye withdraw yourselves from every brother that walks disorderly and not after the tradition they received of us—And if any man obeyeth not our word—note that man and *have no company with him to the end that he may be ashamed.*

It is hoped that even this biblical action would be carried out with the prayer that the Holy Spirit would use it to bring shame, pressure, and ultimately restoration and change.

In the event of demonstrated repentance and desire to return to membership on the part of the dismissed member, the same procedure for those seeking membership will be followed.

---

1. Of course, the church recognizes that one may renounce the jurisdiction of Christ's church by apostasy (I John 2:19). In such cases, if withdrawal during discipline occurs, the church will find it necessary to declare the former member ''apostate.''—ed.

SAMPLE OF A LETTER TO A LAWYER

Dear Mr. _____ :

We do appreciate your interest in _____ and what you have attempted to do in writing to us. That the church's action has upset her we can well realize. However, many of the things you have said in your letter indicate that there is a very real lack of understanding on your part of the pertinent facts in this matter.

First of all, the final decision to disfellowship _____ was not made quickly or without much serious discussion and thought. It came after many months of difficult attempts in trying to help _____ _____ and with suggestions for counseling for one or both, which may have helped if it had been followed through. A log was kept of phone calls, meetings, etc., and finally presented to the whole church body before the decision was made. It must be recognized that on the basis of all the facts the whole congregation voted on the action to remove _____ _____ from fellowship. It was not the isolated act of a few people. Our church constitution states that no member can be allowed to live in an unreconciled state as far as another member is concerned. This we adhere to and it is agreed upon together when a person is voted into membership. We cannot change this, nor do we wish to. Our church operates on historic Baptist principles, which are essentially biblical principles, and include the whole process of church discipline outlined in Matthew chapter 18. The shifts and changes of secular law and pragmatism do not take precedence over these.

Another factor that enters in is that _____ was involved with another family which was breaking up and the whole thing became very complicated. In attempting to meet with _____ to clarify matters and get more insight we were refused a meeting and _____ _____ would not so much as come to give any explanations or information. _____ would not meet with the board, which would have been the courteous and proper thing to do. This involves sensitive matters about others we would not discuss here, but _____ _____ is aware of them.

Another significant factor is that _____ resigned from church membership, that is, attempted to withdraw from us. The whole congregation voted not to accept her letter of withdrawal, but rather to act in disfellowshipping her, which is not an unusual procedure. The fact is that she initiated severance. This is all in the permanent records of the church.

As far as "threatening to advise other fundamental churches that the behavior of _____ made her unworthy of membership," there was never any such thing done. _____ knows that when a person moves his membership to another church it is standard procedure for the receiving church to write to the former requesting a letter of dismissal. In keeping with ethics and honesty, the church will report if the person or persons left in good standing and, if not, will state the circumstances of his leaving. Again, this is standard church procedure that she knows about. I am sure if you were hiring an employee you would expect as much from his former employer. We at Laurelton Park Baptist Church believe that church membership is a sacred and solemn responsibility and the duties are not to be taken lightly. At any rate, no such threats were ever made and _____ was always approached with the sincere desire to see her won back and reconciled. However, she is aware of church procedure and knows that disfellowship is the final step when reconciliation has been rejected.

As we see it, there is nothing different in the situation now than when the church acted to not accept the withdrawal but to disfellowship _____.

We do hope this sheds some further light on the situation and helps you to see that it was not easy for us, given all the factors involved, and that we are being perfectly consistent with our constitution and our rules of membership.

We consider the matter closed.

Sincerely,

Pastor & board members

THE KEY TO THE CASEBOOK

Jay E. Adams

CASE NO. 5 (Page 10 in the *Casebook*)

"I HEARD GOD'S VOICE TELLING ME TO GO TO AFRICA"

"You say that they had you arrested when you tried to force your way on to an airliner headed for Africa?" "Yes—and I'm going to get there yet! I know I was wrong in trying to serve God as I did. I now know that I should have earned the money for my ticket instead of acting so impulsively upon His call. But God has called me to Africa. I know that. I heard His voice as clearly as I hear yours right now. And this was after three days of continuous earnest prayer to discover what God wanted me to do with my life. Surely then, it could not have been of the devil." Twenty-three-year-old Richard, a seminary student, who had never acted erratically before, who was a fine student, and who seemed doctrinally sound, suddenly raced out of his room, hailing a taxi to the airport. Fleeing from the taxi without paying the cabbie, he escaped into the crowd, only to be arrested when insisting that he be allowed to board—without a ticket—a Florida-bound plane that he claimed was headed for Africa.

This case was included to teach the importance of considering the influence of unsuspected secondary factors on behavior. Note the background facts:

1. Richard was a stable student.
2. Richard was doctrinally sound and a fine student.
3. Richard had never acted erratically before.

Now, note the setting for the incident:

1. Richard had been concerned about his calling.
2. Richard had prayed earnestly and continually for three days.

It was this change that occasioned the erratic behavior, which was:

1. He claimed to hear God's voice telling him to go to Africa.
2. He called a taxi and headed for the airport.
3. He did not pay his taxi fare.

42

4. He tried to board a Florida-bound plane without a ticket, claiming it was going to Africa.
5. He was arrested.

Now,

1. He is still convinced that he heard a call.
2. He is still determined to go to Africa.
3. He knows he should pay the taxi driver.
4. He knows that his behavior was "impulsive" regarding the airline.

Is Richard now OK? No. First of all, he has been thinking and acting on the basis of three days of sleep loss. In some persons, two and a half (or more) days of significant REM (Rapid Eye Movement) sleep loss can lead to every effect of LSD. This seems to be what happened to Richard. You can tell from his behavior that he was "out of it," probably hallucinating. The behavior with the taxi driver and at the airport indicates this. So, he must be warned that his so-called revelation from God is equally suspect. When he insists "I heard His voice as clearly as I hear yours right now," you may say to him, "Yes, and you were equally sure that the plane was headed for Africa." He must be told about the effects of sleep loss and convinced not to determine his future on the basis of this supposed voice from heaven.

Secondly, he must be urged to pay the taxi driver, seek forgiveness from the airline, etc.

Thirdly, he must be warned against an extended period of sleepless nights. According to the gospel records, Jesus never missed more than one whole night's sleep at any time.

Fourthly, having made this clear, the counselor must help him to set up and follow a more biblical process for determining his future (cf. my *More than Redemption*, pp. 23-34).

Along the way:

1. His zeal to obey God may rightly be commended.
2. If he is not yet totally reasonable when you speak with him, get him to go to bed for a full day before you talk again.
3. Don't discuss content at outset. Wait until he is sure of what happened before doing so.
4. Relate I Corinthians 6:19, 20; II Corinthians 6:16; and Romans 12:12 to pushing the body beyond its limits.

In cases of bizarre behavior always check *first* for sleep loss or drugs. These are the two most common causes of erratic thinking and action. The solution to the first is a good sleep binge. Only *after* the person has made up his sleep loss should you try to counsel him.

Medicine and Health

BOB SMITH
Editor

Bob Smith is a practicing physician in Lafayette, Indiana, who also works closely with the Christian Counseling Center in that city.

Irritable Bowel Syndrome

In preparation for writing the various articles in this section of the *Journal,* I spend considerable time searching current medical literature for the most up-to-date information on the topics selected. The following article was discovered in the search.[1] It is written in the style of a physician answering questions about the irritable bowel syndrome from a patient. At the conclusion, I will make some remarks about counseling patients with this problem.

1. *Doctor, you say I have irritable bowel syndrome. Other doctors have given me other names for the same problem. What does irritable bowel syndrome mean?*

A. Irritable bowel syndrome is a name we use for any of several conditions for which we can find no physical explanation, no organic cause. Most of the other names for these conditions are less appropriate because they include the word "colitis," which means inflammation of the colon. For example, there's spastic colitis, mucous colitis, cathartic colitis. There is no inflammation in the irritable bowel syndrome. Other names imply even worse problems—colonic neurosis, intestinal neurosis. Irritable bowel syndrome is perhaps the best name we have to describe a problem in the digestive tract involving abdominal pain, bloating, and irregular bowel habits (constipation and/or diarrhea). These are often accompanied by one or more other symptoms such as abdominal rumbling and gurgling, belching, a bad taste in the mouth, loss of appetite, heartburn, nausea, vomiting.

2. *Is irritable bowel syndrome very common?*

A. It is probably the most common disorder of the digestive tract in this country, and in most other developed countries in the world. It accounts for

---

30 to 50 percent of all digestive conditions seen in doctors' offices. The irritable bowel syndrome is almost as frequent a cause of people staying home from work as is the common cold. About twice as many women as men are affected, and even children develop this disorder. Irritable bowel syndrome occurs among all types of people, all income levels, and in all walks of life; however, the people who are most likely to have it are those who are exposed to sustained anxiety and nervous tension.

3. *If it is my colon that is causing the trouble, why do I have pain in different parts of my abdomen at different times?*

A. In order to understand the answer to this question, you must know the anatomy of the colon. It starts in the right lower portion of the abdomen and rises (the ascending colon) to a point just below the right rib cage. The colon then makes a sharp turn and goes left across the abdomen (the transverse colon) to a point just below the left rib cage.Taking another sharp turn the colon continues down the left abdomen (the descending colon) into the lower left portion of the abdomen, where it becomes the sigmoid colon, so-called because of the S-shape it assumes from this point down to the rectum and then to the anus. Thus it is easy to understand why you might have colonic pain in any part of the abdomen or just below the rib cage, and that the pain could change position. You can even have pain deep into the pelvis; the transverse colon is often large, and sometimes hangs far down into the pelvis.

4. *Why do I have so much pain?*

A. Pain is probably caused by excessive muscular contraction—cramping— that produces a localized distension of the colon just behind the contraction. Further distension is due to trapped gas. There is a considerable amount of pressure present in these areas of distension, and the pressure produces a painful bowel.

The pain of irritable bowel syndrome is by far the most common and most important complaint of the patient. It may vary in severity from an indefinite sensation of bloating and distension to severe, cramping pain located through-out the abdomen; it is more pronounced in both sides of the lower abdomen. Pain is intermittent and rhythmic, and becomes much worse at the time of increased colon activity, which is primarily in the early morning and after meals. The pain may be so severe that, if located in the left upper abdomen, it may resemble a heart attack, or, when situated in the right upper abdomen, it may suggest gallbladder disease or even a kidney stone.

The gastrointestinal tract

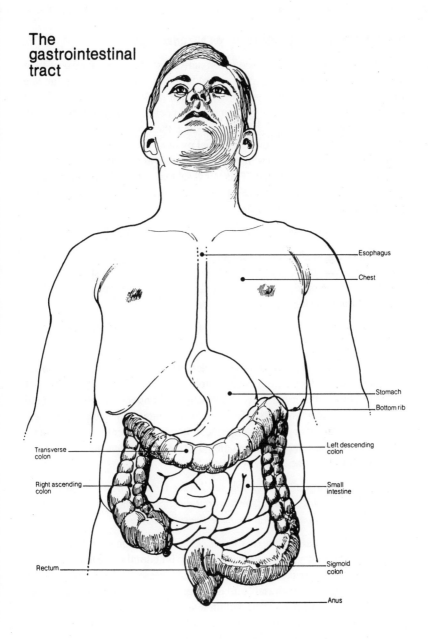

Esophagus

Chest

Stomach

Bottom rib

Transverse colon

Left descending colon

Right ascending colon

Small intestine

Rectum

Sigmoid colon

Anus

5. *Why do the attacks often come on just after a meal?*

A. Because there is increased colon activity at that time. Intake of food stimulates the release of gastrointestinal hormones, which in turn stimulate intestinal muscles. Many experts believe that these hormones, gastrin and cholecystokinin, contribute to the increase in colon activity in patients with irritable bowel syndrome, and thus produce their symptoms. We have no real proof of that, but the circumstantial evidence is good. A bowel movement often relieves the abdominal pain following meals, especially for patients who are constipated. This suggests that symptoms result from the normal action of one or more of the digestive tract hormones upon the unusually sensitive gut muscles.

6. *Would you please tell me exactly what the colon does?*

A. Primarily, it absorbs water and, to a lesser extent, minerals, from the wastes received from the small intestine. It also stores the stool, enabling you to defecate more or less on schedule rather than after each meal, when the small intestine has completed its work.

7. *If there is nothing organically wrong with me, why does my colon keep acting up?*

A. You have overactive bowel muscles that are causing abnormal bowel contractions. That's the fundamental problem in all patients with any type of irritable bowel: abnormal bowel contractions. Contractions of the sigmoid colon are stronger and more frequent in patients with marked pain and constipation, weaker and less frequent in those patients with diarrhea. Regardless of the symptoms, the colon overreacts to mental stress and many other pressures that occur in everyday life.

8. *I have constipation, and you say I have irritable bowel syndrome. A friend whose doctor told her she has irritable bowel syndrome has diarrhea all the time. Is it possible that we have the same disease?*

A. First, let's define the two terms. Constipation means the infrequent passage of small, dry, hard stools; often there is abdominal distension and/or a lot of gas. In the irritable bowel syndrome, increases in colonic pressure do not noticeably move material from one segment of the colon to another, but rather cause to-and-fro mixing within a segment. Because of these spastic contractions, the stool stays in the colon for a longer than normal period, during which the colon absorbs large amounts of water. As a result, the stool becomes so dehydrated that when it is finally passed, it consists of hard, dry balls. Sometimes, as a consequence of spasm of the sigmoid colon, rectum, and anus, the stool may be narrow and ribbonlike, accounting for the occasional sensation of having an incomplete bowel movement.

A few patients with irritable bowel syndrome complain of diarrhea, either steady or intermittent. Diarrhea means that the stool is a semiliquid and bowel movements are more frequent. In the irritable bowel syndrome, there is often great urgency, the stools may be quite small in volume, and they contain great quantities of mucus; some movements appear to consist of mucus alone. The quiet, underactive bowel speeds the progress of stools; there is little resistance to their flow. When the stool is soft, unformed, and watery, it means that it passed through the colon too rapidly for the normal absorption of water.

Intermittent diarrhea may also be due to unusual bowel contractions. Some authorities describe patients with intermittent diarrhea as having alternate diarrhea and constipation. The stools often pass several times daily, one movement consisting of a small hard pellet of stool and the others of copious clear mucus. Thus, there is a question as to whether these patients have constipation, diarrhea, or both. The cyclic pattern suggests irritable bowel syndrome.

9.   *You mentioned that people who have a lot of anxiety and are nervous are the ones most likely to develop irritable bowel syndrome. How can nerves affect my bowel?*

A.   Emotional makeup plays a major part in the irritable bowel syndrome; stress has been shown to cause either the start or the return of symptoms. Many patients who manifest rapidly alternating constipation and diarrhea have been shown to have patterns of increased and decreased activity of the sigmoid colon that correlate well with their moods. In these patients, decreased colon activity and diarrhea correlated well with depression, while constipation related to anxiety.

The many normal problems, frustrations, and anxieties of everyday life—fear of disease, a change in life conditions, a new job, unexpected loss of money or work, and fatigue—rather than psychiatric disorders seem to trigger the symptoms of irritable bowel syndrome. The overall conclusion, therefore, has been that functional disturbances charactistic of the irritable colon are normal manifestations of emotional tension. Just as shame causes blushing, fear causes contraction or spasm of a segment of gut. This in turn causes abdominal pain and, if the tension is prolonged or intense, constipation or diarrhea. Understanding and accepting the emotional components of these symptoms sometimes promote relief.

10.   *Can an ulcer affect the colon?*

A.   Yes, indeed. This is known as the secondary irritable bowel syndrome. Patients may have associated problems such as duodenal ulcer, heartburn, gallbladder disease, Crohn's disease, ulcerative colitis, or diverticulitis. In fact, the irritable bowel syndrome has been associated with diverticulosis and diverticulitis. Diverticula are essentially outpocketings in the wall of the colon, and diverticulitis is the result of blockage and inflammation of one of these pouches. One of the causes of diverticulosis is thought to be increased pressure in the colon, and this increased pressure is especially noted in irritable bowel syndrome.

The reason a physician puts his patient through all sorts of lab tests and X-ray studies is to rule out organic problems that may be present along with the irritable bowel syndrome. If any other organic problem such as an ulcer is found, both it and the secondary irritable bowel syndrome will have to be treated in order to achieve success.

11.   *I've read about fiber in the newspapers and magazines, and they say that everyone should be eating it. Could you tell me exactly what fiber is and how it works?*

A.   The big word in diet these days is roughage—dietary fiber—which refers to all foods that reach the colon essentially unchanged. Food fiber comes from plants; grains, vegetables, fruits, nuts, and seeds contain varying amounts of roughage. Vegetable dietary fiber acts principally on the colon. Its absorptive ability varies according to the variety of fruit or vegetable. Meat, fish, poultry, and dairy products contain no dietary fiber whatsoever, although you should, of course, include them in your diet for their protein and nutrients.

Some long-term studies have demonstrated that increased dietary fiber produces a bulkier stool and reduces tension in the walls of the descending colon. Patients with irritable bowel syndrome who eat high-fiber foods often have less pain. Patients who complain of constipation—whether or not they have diverticulosis—should increase their dietary fiber intake to tolerance limits, with the hope that it will improve their symptoms.

The high-fiber diet helps both the patient with predominant constipation and the patient with predominant diarrhea. In the patient with constipation, small rock-hard stools become larger, softer, and more easily passed; in the patient with diarrhea, the stools absorb the water that was previously passed as watery diarrhea.

12.   *What can be done to cure me of the irritable bowel syndrome?*

A.   There is no absolute cure. Although some spontaneous cures have been reported, most investigators emphasize that symptoms return over a span of many years. With continual treatment, however, most patients have an excellent chance of staying relatively pain-free. And it is interesting that threatment for the syndrome involves trips to the grocery store and the water fountain rather than to the pharmacy.

Start on a high-fiber diet and each day add 1 tablespoon of miller's bran mixed with cereals or soups, or baked into muffins or cookies. Add an additional tablespoonful every three to four days until you're getting four tablespoonfuls daily. On very rare occasions, this diet may initially intensify symptoms, but this effect is only temporary. A reasonable aim of this diet is to enable you to have one or two bulky, semiformed stools daily. If you find that you require dietary fiber over and above your daily intake, add a bland bulk additive, such as psyllium preparation [Konsyl, Metamucil, Mondane Bulk, etc.], stirring one rounded teaspoonful into a glass of cold water, juice, or other liquid one to three times a day. For best results, follow each dose with an additional glass of liquid. Drink plenty of water—perhaps six to eight glasses daily—in addition to fluids taken with meals; this will greatly influence the consistency of the stool and the frequency of bowel action.

This treatment will probably help you; it is suitable for the majority of patients. While very few become and remain symptom-free, many nonetheless obtain considerable relief.

13.   *I don't understand, Doctor. I've always been told to stay away from foods with a lot of roughage. Now you tell me just the opposite!*

A.   The bland, low-residue, non-roughage diet recommended only a few years ago for patients with irritable bowel syndrome is now being replaced by a high-fiber diet following reports of relief of spasm and pain after switching to such a diet. Although the syndrome has been around for many years, only in recent times has its cause and treatment been understood.

14.   *Specifically, which foods contain a lot of fiber, and how much is enough?*

A.   Among the plant foods high in fiber are whole wheat and bran cereals, peas, beans, carrots, turnips, peaches, apples, whole oranges, pears, raisins, and prunes. The best sources are miller's bran and packaged bran cereals. The high-fiber theory is so new that no recommended daily allowance for fiber has yet been established. The need varies with the individual, and the effect of the added fiber upon your bowel movements is the best guide. If the amount of roughage eaten does not produce regular bowel movements, add a little more. If the reverse is true, cut it down.

15. *But, Doctor, I hurt. What can I do for relief during an attack?*

A.   Apply a heating pad or hot water bottle after meals; this often relieves the abdominal pain and possibly reduces the increased activity of the bowel. During acute attacks, avoid gas-forming vegetables such as onions, beans, and those in the cabbage family, including brussels sprouts, cauliflower, and broccoli. Fried foods and fresh fruit may also upset the stomach at this time. As your symptoms resolve, it is important to resume the high-fiber diet.

Doctors generally do not advise injections with pain relievers during an attack. To relieve constipation, don't use laxatives or enemas; these irritate the colon more.

16. *Does this disease cause cancer?*

A.   To date, there is absolutely no conclusive evidence to link irritable bowel syndrome to any type of cancer, although a recent study suggests that over half the patients have such a fear. Studies also suggest that diverticular disease is twice as common in persons with histories of irritable bowel syndrome as in the general population. There is also an increased incidence of hemorrhoids and anal fissures, due to constipation.

Concluding Comments

The answer to question 9 is one of interest to biblical counselors. In describing the relationship between problems and life and symptoms of irritable bowel syndrome, the author blames "emotional make-up." Another author more correctly states, "The symptoms of Irritable Bowel Syndrome tend to occur as a reaction to stress. . . ."[2]

When patients first come in, they will give you many small clues to their underlying nervousness. Patients with irritable bowel syndrome will claim to be the calmest, most non-reactive persons in the world; at the same time you may notice that they have a nervous cough or tic, or constantly wring their hands. Sweaty palms and excessive leg movements are also certain

2. William D. Davis, Jr., M.D., "Lower Bowel Disorders, 1. Irritable Bowel Syndrome," *Post Graduate Medicine* 68, 4 (October 1980):60-64.

giveaways to the tense patient who claims to be under control at all times.

You need to find out about the types of stresses the patient is encountering in everyday life, but be careful about how you probe for them. If you ask the patient if she is under stress, it puts her in an unfair position. First, not everyone is aware of what is stressful to her. Second, the stress doesn't immediately trigger a response of pain, diarrhea, and constipation. Instead, most people's immediate response will handle the stress at that time. It is only after the stress is over—a period of hours, days, or sometimes even longer—that it begins to affect them.

People can often tolerate an intense degree of stress for short periods, whereas repeated stress, the "Chinese water torture," day-by-day stress, can lead to symptoms. Having feelings of being trapped in a job or a life situation or having an intense sense of obligation may produce the repeated stress that leads to the irritable bowel. Patients often do not recognize this kind of stress because they believe their doctor is asking about something that happened to them the day the pain developed. It requires a careful history to bring out past or continuing stresses that can be responsible for the presenting symptoms. Finally, take a job history; it may provide information about both work stress and symptom-producing chemicals exposure (lead toxicity).

If the patients have intermittent symptoms, I ask them to give me a log of a "good day" and a "bad day." They describe their activities, meals, and symptoms for a 24-hour period beginning from the time they arise. The log can show, for example, how meals trigger symptoms.

If I were permitted to ask only one question to determine whether the complaint were functional[3] or organic,[4] I would ask, "Do your symptoms awaken you at night?" It's very important how you ask this question. There is a very real difference between awakening *with* pain and being awakened *by* the pain. For example, depressed persons have early morning insomnia— they awaken at 4, 5, and 6 in the morning and then begin to feel pain or other somatic[5] complaints. If pain or diarrhea at night repeatedly awakens the patient suspected to have irritable bowel syndrome, the possibility of a functional etiology is much less likely.[6]

In his answer to question 9, the author has concluded that "understanding

---

3. Not due to diseases but physical responses to problems in life.
4. Actual diseases in the body.
5. Physical or bodily.
6. Marvin M. Schuster, M.D., "Irritable Bowel Syndrome," *Diagnosis* 1, 4 (September/October 1979):70-75.

and accepting the emotional components of these symptoms sometimes promote relief." This points to one of the benefits of biblical counseling. More than understanding is available for believers. As a person evaluates the various difficulties of life, he reaches a certain conclusion about that difficulty. If the conclusion is unbiblical, a physical response will be produced. "Just as shame causes blushing, fear causes contraction or spasm of a segment of gut [or bowel]. This in turn causes abdominal pain." By responding to the difficulty in a biblical way, the resulting symptoms of unbiblical response may be avoided. Thus a counselor may help a person reduce the frequency and severity of symptoms and conceivably experience complete cessation of symptoms. But change in symptoms cannot be the primary goal. A person must respond to problems in a biblical manner even if and when there is no change in physical symptoms.

Medical News of Interest
To the Nouthetic Counselor

OBESITY IN CHILDHOOD

"There is no single, clear-cut . . . answer to why a child becomes obese." By the time help is sought for these children, "the situation has been out of control for a long time. Typically, they come from families in which the father and perhaps one or two siblings[1] can eat like horses yet remain thin as rails. The mother, on the other hand, is a person who is constantly fighting a weight problem. Alternatively, the entire family is overweight.

"The physiological and emotional components of overeating vary from one child to the next. Children who come from families that overeat tend to follow the same pattern, often because eating is the most gratifying activity the family can share.

"In these cases, the parents may not have the time, energy, or money to entertain their children with active recreation, and they may regard food as one important satisfaction they can offer them. Others find that they can most easily identify with overweight family members by overeating and becoming obese themselves."

The article continues, speculating that "sometimes children overeat to express anger and rebellion against one or both parents. This may be true in cases in which the mother is constantly nagging a child to lose weight or in which the child's needs for attention and encouragement are not being met.[2] Children regard eating as a way of giving something to themselves because they feel deprived of other things.

"Parents often feel that they are not being good providers unless their children are round, chubby babies. This can establish a pattern of overeating."[3]

---

1. Brothers or sisters.
2. Note the emphasis on supposed need satisfaction.—ed.
3. *Family Practice News* 11, 6:3, 72.

INFANT MORTALITY

"The nation's infant mortality continued to decline last year to a record low of 12.5 deaths per 1,000 live births." In 1979, this figure was 13.0 deaths per 1,000 live births.

"The birth rate rose nearly 4% over the preceding year to a rate of 16.2 live births per 1,000 population, or 69.2 live births per 1,000 women aged 15-44 years. The rise reflected a continued growth in the number of women of childbearing age and an increase in the childbearing rate.

"The marriage rate, which has risen each year since 1977, was 10.9 per 1,000 population for a total of 2,413,000 marriages, the most ever recorded in the country. The divorce rate held steady at 5.3 per 1,000, for a total of 1,182,000 divorces."[4]

UNRESTRAINED CHILDREN AND AUTOMOBILE COLLISIONS

"Driving with an unrestrained child can lead to an automobile collision." A study was conducted of "at least 554 collisions in which an unrestrained child was the direct cause and 194 cases in which the child was at least a contributing factor.

"It was judged that 52.4% of the 748 collisions involving children definitely could have been prevented had the children been restrained in some manner.

"The type of child behavior leading to collisions varied and included: 329 instances when the child fell onto the floor of the car, on the driver, out of the window or door, or from the rear of a truck; 117 in which the child grabbed the gears or the steering wheel or crawled onto the driver's lap; 57 in which the driver attended to the child; and 41 in which the driver failed to take defensive or evasive action and instead grabbed the child.

"The improper use of crash-tested child restraint devices resulted in 24 collisions, stressing that improper use of these devices can severely limit their accident preventive value.

"Besides these collisions involving moving cars, 142 collisions happened when children knocked parked cars into gear or released the parking brake. Children, restrained or unrestrained, should not be left alone in a car."

---

4. *Family Practice News* 11, 10:19.

The investigators recommended "that it be stressed to parents that children need to be restrained while in the car and that restraints must be installed correctly and used properly if they are to be of any value. Children large enough to sit up by themselves should use seat belts, which should have the same collision preventive value as restraint devices."[5]

CHILD ABUSE AND TEENAGE PREGNANCY

A recent survey shows that "child abuse occurs more often in families where the mothers had teenage pregnancies and children were born out of wedlock.

"Children who were born out of wedlock were 2.5 times more likely to be abused than other children."[6]

DIVORCE AND CHILDREN

"Government statistics show that fully one-third of all children alive today in the United States will have their parents separate or divorce by the time they are 18 years old—approximately 1 million children each year."[7]

HEADACHE IN CHILDREN

"From 5% to 10% of school-age children have migraines.

"The throbbing and pounding pain of migraine headache is frequently severe enough to interfere with usual activities." The pain will seem to be in the front or on both sides of the head, except in teenagers and young adults, in whom these headaches tend to be more on one side of the head. "They may last for days, and are frequently experienced on waking in the morning.

"The tension headache, on the other hand, usually does not disrupt normal activities. It often erupts as a dull pain in a band-like sensation, although it can involve the whole head.

"Heredity is not a consideration, as it is with migraines, psychogenic factors. Tense, nervous persons are the most commonly affected.

5. *Family Practice News* 11, 9:10.
6. *Family Practice News* 11, 8:41.
7. *Family Practice News* 11, 6:3.

"In migraine headaches, the best treatment is frequently none. If they occur only three or four times a year, bed rest and sleep may be recommended."[8]

SUICIDE AND THE AGED

"Suicide among the elderly is rapidly on the rise, attributable in part to society's and psychiatry's indulgence of the hopelessness and depression that afflict so many elderly persons.

"Society and the psychiatric community appear to believe the false and insidious notion that 'life is essentially over' for persons older than 60 or 65." The writer goes on to say that they "should instead be bending every effort to make life as stimulating and meaningful as possible for the elderly.

"In 1977, those over the age of 60 constituted 18.3% of the United States population, but they accounted for 23% of suicidal deaths. Suicide among elderly males was particularly high. Males appear to be prone to a greater degree of disorientation and life change in old age, although studies show that elderly women suffer more from depression.

"Elderly men and women also make more serious attempts at suicide than persons in younger age groups.

"Suicidal elderly patients are more likely to have some physical illness or debilitation; be institutionalized or dependent on others; be retired; take multiple medications, including anti-depressants; be prone to paranoia; be withdrawn; and have lost the capacity to seek stimulation.

"In the long term, society must redefine its views on the aging process and eradicate its bipolar attitude which keeps the elderly alive as long as possible, but accepts and even exacerbates their loss of hope and meaning in life."[9]

MENOPAUSAL SYMPTOMS

"The majority of symptoms associated with menopause are psychosocial or cultural in origin and respond as significantly to placebo therapy as to estrogen replacement therapy."[10] This is saying that most of the menopausal

---

8. *Family Practice News* 11, 12:42.
9. *Family Practice News* 11, 12:2, 54.
10. *Family Practice News* 11, 11:19.

symptoms are the results of what a woman has learned in her home and environment and also the result of her responses to stresses in life. As a result, when these women are given pills that contain no medication, they respond as well as women who are given actual estrogen therapy. If their problem was due to hormone lack, there would be a significant improvement on estrogen therapy with no help received from the placebo therapy.

WIVES OF HEAVY SMOKERS

"Wives of heavy smokers have a higher risk of developing and dying of lung cancer than wives of nonsmokers or light smokers.

"Husbands' smoking habits did not appear to affect their wives' risk of dying from other diseases, such as stomach cancer, cervical cancer, or heart disease. The risk of developing emphysema and asthma was slightly higher in the nonsmoking wives of heavy smokers.

"These results emerged from a study of 91,540 nonsmoking married women aged 40 and above who were followed for 14 years (1966–1979). The husbands of 21,895 women were nonsmokers or only occasionally smoked.

"The wives of heavy smokers had a twofold increased risk of dying of lung cancer over that of wives of men who were nonsmokers.

"These results indicate the possible importance of passive, or indirect, smoking as one of the causal factors of lung cancer and cast doubt on the practice of assessing the relative risk of developing lung cancers in smokers solely by comparing them with nonsmokers."[11]

PREGNANCY AND EXERCISE

"Excessive exercise during pregnancy can be harmful to both mother and fetus, but moderate activity is usually not harmful.

"Sports such as scuba diving, long distance running, and climbing at altitudes above 10,000 feet should be avoided because of the risk of hypoia."[12]

Exercise increases the amount of work that the heart must do as well as the heart rate and "decreases the blood flow to the uterus, thereby decreasing the supply of oxygen to the fetus.

---

11. *Family Practice News* 11, 6:4.
12. Low oxygen in the bloodstream.

"Work is also an activity that should be monitored carefully.

"One activity that can continue uninterrupted during pregnancy is coitus,"[13] provided there are no complications involved in the pregnancy at that point.

KARATE INJURIES

"Competitors in karate matches should be required to wear protective padding to prevent serious injuries.

"There should be less emphasis on the skills that are most likely to result in injury, such as breaking wood with the hands.

"Injuries were most common in the limbs, due to repeated kicks absorbed by the legs and breaking of wood by the hands. Wood breaking results in grotesque deformities of the hand and possible subsequent damage to the joints."[14]

PATIENTS' MEMORY
OF PHYSICIAN'S INSTRUCTIONS

"Not much more than 60% of what the patient is told will be remembered for more than 4 weeks. Patients may forget a significant amount of what they are told within 10 minutes after speaking to their physician. Studies show that when the advice is mentioned first during the conversation, the recall rate is about 75%; this is a better recall rate than occurs when the advice is mentioned midway during the coversation or even when the physician stresses the importance of the advice given.

"One way of improving recall is by providing written material for patients. The reading should be no higher than the eighth grade; studies demonstrate that many patients will not understand material written at a more sophisticated level.

"The physician should be specific. When counseling the obese patient about dieting, for instance, the results will be better if the patient is instructed to 'cut excess fat off the meat,' instead of just 'eat less fat.' "[15]

---

13. *Family Practice News* 11, 10:42.
14. *Family Practice News* 11, 10:27.
15. *Family Practice News* 11, 6:74.

If physicians have problems helping patients recall their instructions, it is very likely nouthetic counselors will have the same difficulty. Counselors need to be as specific in their instructions as a physician is in his and not fail to give clear, written homework.

BEHAVIOR AND FOOD COLORINGS

"Artificial food colorings do not affect the behavior of school-age children who are said to be sensitive to these agents."

A study was conducted which was "designed to maximize the likelihood of demonstrating the behavioral effect of artificial food colorings. Only children already on the Feingold diet and who were reported by their parents to respond markedly to artificial food colorings were studied. Placebo responders were excluded from the study and high dosages of food coloring were administered.

"The children consumed artificially colored cookies for one week and cookies with natural ingredients, as recommended by the Feingold diet, for another week. A one-week washout period was interposed between the two experimental periods to insure that the child returned to baseline levels.

"Clinically, most of the children did not react dramatically to either type of cookie, contrary to the expectations of their parents. They were evaluated for behavioral changes by parents, teachers, psychiatrists, and psychologists. None of the ratings demonstrated significant differences between placebo and artificial colorings.

"Teacher, parent, psychiatrist and child were asked to guess the type of cookie at the end of each trial week. None guessed, beyond chance, the type of cookie. The older children in the test were studied for distractibility. No dietary effects were demonstrated.

"Most of the children did not meet the usual criteria for hyperactivity. No dietary effects were demonstrated, however, even in children clearly diagnosable as hyperactive."[16]

---

16. *Family Practice News* 11, 12:52.

Missions

MILTON FISHER
Editor

Milton Fisher is professor of Old Testament and president of the Reformed Episcopal Seminary, Philadelphia. He was formerly a missionary to Ethiopia.

You Never Had It So Tough

No church buildings allowed. No public advertising possible. No full-time pastors available. No street meetings or neighborhood crusades permitted. No permits for local radio broadcasting available. Instead—close surveillance and restrictive opposition to contend with. How can you expect to start or build up churches under such conditions? Would you personally consider a call to give it a try? I've got to be kidding?

No, I'm not kidding. I'm just describing conditions as we found them on a recent visit to Morocco, the conditions under which the North Africa Mission is seriously attempting to fulfill a faith-commitment to see 25 churches planted among the five nations to which its witness is directed. Not an easy task! With man it would be impossible; with God all things are possible. A specially arranged tour for delegates on the way to NAM's Centennial conference at Viviers, in Provence (southern France), gave me the opportunity to see how it is done. And what a blessing it was to see God at work in so difficult a place. What glory is due His name for His Spirit's life-giving power.

Fez, one of the oldest centers of Islamic studies in the world, certainly in North Africa, is a good place to start. We reached there by chartered bus, from Casablanca via Marrakech. Still operative there are a couple of *medrassas* ("universities") which date back twelve hundred years, to the early centuries of Muslim conquest. Throughout medieval and modern times Muslim leaders have assembled at these centers to study Islamics and to indoctrinate the succeeding generation. Interestingly, that was the one town visited by us where all the Christians we met were male, *young* men at that. One leading Christian witness in the city is a Middle Eastern Arab. He runs a business operation, to legitimatize his presence, but his zeal for the gospel is irrepressible. There is no formal church organized as yet, but several earnest youths are being discipled to that end.

One evening we met with six of these young men in a home, within walking distance of our hotel. Small talk at the opening of our conversation included their own description of their city. "In Fez," said one, "between

67

one mosque and another—there is another mosque!" One of the men is a teacher of English, so he was largely spokesman for the group. He in fact entertained us for a while by telling "Jeeha stories," simple little folk tales with a surprise ending or punch line. When the talk turned to the serious side, there was an interesting turnabout. Instead of our listening to how each of them was brought to Christ, they wanted to hear *our* testimonies.

Later, these young believers were asked to give us their prayer requests. This was not just to prepare for an immediate season of prayer, though we did indeed have prayer together, but that we might bring these pressing needs to the attention of the body of Christ here at home. As you would expect, some of those requests "run deep"; they should provoke us to serious thought and earnest prayer. The Muslim Brotherhood and other zealots, noted one, have been holding Islamic conferences for the express purpose of fostering opposition and repression of all Christian witness. Another spoke of a seemingly Satanic attack on the health of his family of late. One very moving request came from the father of a seven-year-old boy. The child's mother and grandparents are staunch Muslims. The lad must attend an Islamic school. Consequently, apart from the teaching privately given by his father, he is totally immersed in a Muslim environment. "Pray," he begged us, "that God's Spirit will convince the boy of the truth, in the face of so much pressure from error." On a more positive note, one young brother wanted us to give thanks with him for his newfound liberty and courage in witnessing to his faith in Christ with a power unknown to him when he first believed. His testimony was that now his wife is saved, his entire family knows of his Christian faith, and his brother now attends meetings to learn for himself. Another fellow made a particularly bold and significant request. He asked that we all be praying that God may somehow use someone in a position of authority in the government of his nation to pave the way to greater freedom for Christian belief, practice, and witness.

What impressed me most throughout our visit was the moral fiber of these woefully isolated believers. "Hopeless" as their cause may seem at first, one is suddenly struck by the realization that we are not really dealing with a tiny group of helpless and fearful rejects from society, but with a dynamic core of enthusiastically courageous believers in the lordship of Christ the King. They KNOW that theirs is NOT a lost cause; their task is difficult but not impossible, in Him. They long and pray for Christ to manifest His glory and might, and they only seek the *how* to be made plain.

Not once, in fact, at Fez, at Casablanca, Marrakech or Rabat, did we sense an air of defeatism—not even one of feeling sorry for themselves. A most striking example of this was when 14-year-old Bushra ("Good News") was asked whether she had many Christian friends her own age. She smiled sweetly and in perfectly clear English remarked, "I have no close friends." Her parents had given up the opportunity to emigrate for the sake of greater freedom in favor of purchasing a larger home—a former Jewish residence and synagogue! That home is now "Number Two" of the 25 new churches being sought in the region. The recent baptism of Fatima, mother of three lovely little children, made her husband eligible for eldership, fulfilling a requirement for church status for that local congregation.

Throughout the Muslim world today it is not advisable to give an openly aggressive witness at one's place of employment or at school (some, like attractive Maria Mulay, are now at university level). That would be tantamount to asking for it—for termination. After all, to the majority of Muslims, loyalty to the national religion is more a matter of patriotism than it is of personal spirituality. Nevertheless, the Christian can and must LIVE his faith under ANY circumstance. When *this* "peculiar" life of honesty, decency, and love raises questions about the *difference*, then a calm witness for Christ comes as an acquiescence to someone's curiosity, rather than an affront. It is at the same time the most effective kind of testimony.

Speaking of testimony and the prospect of persecution, one of our newfound Christian brothers, named Omar Z., observed that in his opinion half the persecution suffered was "our own fault." If a measure of discretion is shown, things need not be all that bad. And Omar knows whereof he speaks as a matter of experience. He has attended conferences of "ex-Muslims" at various locations, including Cyprus and India, with a stopover in Egypt. In India he was careful to use his less Arabic sounding patronym, to avoid discrimination there. In Egypt he found the treatment of Bible-believing converts from Islam to be worse than back home. "Here in Morocco," he assured us, "at least the police will protect you from harm, even though they may question you out of duty. There is a degree of tolerance, *if* you are discreet in your life and witness. You don't even have to call yourself "Christian," a term of highly distorted and charged content for the Muslim (as with Jews), but a believer in Jesus Christ as the Son of God. Those too may be "fighting words" to the average Muslim, but that confession lies at the heart of true theology and faith. It stands as more of a challenge to discussion than as a personal affront.

The question raised most frequently by westerners is how a former Muslim ever moved in the direction of belief in Christ, the Christ of the Bible rather than of the Quran. Let young Khalifa tell us his personal story. He was our companion at Fez, as we toured the market and lunched (= dined!) at the home of Mazhar M. Khalifa's progress toward confession of biblical faith was extended over a long enough period of time that one member of our tour group from the States remembered praying for him by name during his struggle over giving in to the Lord. For Khalifa, as perhaps for many, *curiosity* was step one. An Arabic radio program beamed from Europe aroused an interest in Christianity. A one-year Bible correspondence course then gave him more to think about, and a contact by an NAM missionary (who in turn put him in touch with a Moroccan believer) made it personal. He was soon invited to a four-day conference, where about thirty ex-Muslim Christians were assembled. That sent him reeling! He never imagined he'd meet that many local believers. A year later, newly graduated from high school, he attended another conference, where some young Christians from Florida, U.S.A., patiently answered questions and explained some things he needed to know. As he himself testifies, "By then I felt myself CHANGED, daily, Christ taking away evil things from my life." A final 24-hour internal battle brought him to the point of requesting baptism, the crucial step and sign of surrender.

This is not to say that "all is well" or that we find only optimism and encouragement when we view the present state of the Christian church in North Africa. Not all is "rosy" or normal. At Marseilles we met Fatiha, an Algerian believer who is now a nurse. She had arrived from London, where she's currently employed, to attend and help staff the large convention (near 400 attended) for the NAM Centennial (alias Centenary Brit.) at Viviers. She has remained in England following the completion of her training, for if she were to return home as a single woman her family would without doubt arrange for her to be married to a Muslim. A number of female believers have in fact thus dropped into oblivion, as far as any further Christian contacts are concerned. Fatiha was led to Christ by two missionaries from another group but learned English from NAMers. She is very intelligent, witty, and personable, seemingly well able to take care of herself for now. But what of her future?

Recently a young woman in a Moroccan city was so severely harrassed by her postman that she wrote a request that the Bible correspondence lessons be halted. The mail carrier had become suspicious about her regular letters from abroad and had peeked at the contents. Finally he opened one of the letters in her presence, read it aloud to her so that she would know that he knew exactly what it said, then threatened her, "The next time you receive one of these I'll take you *and* the letter straight to the police!" In her cancellation request she spoke of how miserable it made her to resist family and official pressures in the attempt to follow what she believed to be the right way, suggesting that death alone could bring her peace.

Yet God continues to use unexpected means to arouse interest in the true faith of the Scriptures. In recent days the very intensification of opposition has become the means of attracting attention to and inquiry about the Christian message. A Muslim-authored TV series on the prophets of the Old Testament led to an unprecedented number of requests for Bibles. One North African girl wrote to the producers of a gospel radio program that she was pleased to hear "Sweet Hour of Prayer" in her own Arabic language. She had liked that Christian song the first time she'd heard it, in English—on the TV program, "Little House on the Prairie"! A Moroccan man came to faith in Christ by way of radio messages, out of strong disillusionment over the degenerate lives of some supposedly devout Muslims he knew.

As was said earlier, the seeking of the lost sheep and the establishment of churches in an area such as North Africa is not an easy task. Impossible, in fact, in human strength. The hardest part of the work is perhaps the preparation of *our* hearts and lives for positive witness and patient discipling. We can and should increase our efforts, considering that one-sixth of the world's population is Muslim, with only two percent of the Christian missionary force directed toward reaching them.

I close with observations made at the North Africa Mission's centennial convention at Viviers by two English brothers long involved in the efforts of that mission. Howard Stalley said, "Islam has yet to feel the impact of Pentecost," but he was able to report movement in the right direction within the time frame of his own active ministry. During his first nine years on the field he saw only three baptisms; during a second segment of service in North Africa he witnessed nine baptisms in three years—an encouraging turnabout! Ron Wayne, present English home director, drew direct aim at that hardest part, *our* part, of which I spoke just above, when he said, "The Muslim doesn't care how much you know; he wants to know how much you care."

Well, how much?—M.F.

71

Para
Christianity

WESLEY WALTERS
Editor

Wesley Walters is pastor of a congregation in Illinois. For over twenty-five years he has devoted much time to the study of the cults.

Dan Vogel, a former member and missionary of the Church of Jesus Christ of Latter-day Saints, over a year ago made the difficult decision to leave the Mormon Church. He is presently considering the claims of Christianity. Meanwhile he is putting into writing some of the internal conflicts of Mormonism that helped shape his decision to leave the LDS Church. The following article is one of the best discussions we have seen to date on the problems involved in Joseph Smith's claim to have "translated" the *Book of Mormon*. We are pleased to make this material available to readers of the *Journal*.

Is the Book of Mormon
A Translation?

A Response to Edward H. Ashment

DAN VOGEL

How was the *Book of Mormon* translated? Or is it a translation at all? It is essential to answer these questions before any meaningful examination of the *Book of Mormon* is possible, for the way one answers them will determine whether the *Book of Mormon* is seen as authentic history or nineteenth-century fiction.

For the careful reader, the *Book of Mormon* presents many anachronistic problems not confronted by students of authentic historical documents. The historian must question the *Book of Mormon's* claim to be authentic history since its Old Testament portion is literally peppered with hundreds of phrases and quotations from the King James New Testament. To these literary problems is added a theological problem when it is claimed by Joseph Smith and his associates that the supposed "translation" is the result of direct divine communication. This assertion, if true, would make God responsible for the *Book of Mormon's* anachronistic errors. The thousands of grammatical errors in the first edition also, on such a claim, call into question God's perfection.[1] Moreover, Joseph Smith would have to be viewed as a fallen prophet for having made changes in the God-given text of that first edition.

When Mormon apologists became aware of the dilemma of thier church's position, they quickly realized that the old teaching had to be "abandoned" if the *Book of Mormon* were to regain its credibility.[2] This was done by

---

1. For God's perfection in the Bible, see Deut. 32:4; II Sam. 22:31; Job 37:16; Psalms 19:7. And for God's perfection in Mormon scripture, see 2 Ne. 9:20; D&C 38:1, 2; 3:2. Mormon apologist B. H. Roberts admitted that if the translation of the *Book of Mormon* was the result of direct revelation, then God would have to be responsible for the bad grammar. "But," says Roberts, "that is unthinkable, not to say blasphemous." See B. H. Roberts, *Defense of the Faith and the Saints,* 2 vols. (Salt Lake City: The Deseret News, 1907), I:278.

2. Ibid., I:307.

down-playing their church's former position and shifting the emphasis from a strictly divine translation to a more human accomplishment which stressed Joseph Smith's role as translator. So, instead of claiming the *Book of Mormon* was the product of strict, "literal" translation, one in which God revealed in "mechanical" fashion an exact word-for-word translation to the translator, the new hypothesis claimed the *Book of Mormon* is really the product of loose, "conceptual" translation, one in which God supposedly revealed only "concepts" to Smith, and he was left to express them in the best English at his command.[3] Thus, if successfully maintained, this new translation hypothesis would allow Mormon apologists to blame Joseph Smith for the anachronistic and grammatical errors while insisting that the *Book of Mormon* is "conceptually correct. In this manner Mr. Edward H. Ashment would like to explain the *Book of Mormon's* use of New Testament terminology in its Old Testament portion. In his recent *Sunstone* article he regards the New Testament wording as being part of Smith's vocabulary which was drawn upon when using his own words to express the "concepts" on the plates. Furthermore, any changes Smith chose to make in subsequent editions could be explained as refinements which clarified the revealed concepts.

The *conceptual hypothesis* was first discussed at the turn of the century, by Mormon apologist B. H. Roberts, and has gradually gained favor until today it is the position held by nearly all Mormon scholars. Recently these arguments defending this new hypothesis have been assembled by Edward H. Ashment in his article, "The Book of Mormon—A Literal Translation?" *Sunstone*, March–April 1980. Because Ashment's article is representative of Mormon apologetics defending the *conceptual hypothesis,* a response to his article will serve as a response to the Mormon position in general. First, it will be shown that because Ashment cannot adequately deal with the testimonies of Joseph Smith and his associates concerning the *mechanical* and *literal* method of translating the *Book of Mormon,* the *conceptual*

---

3. Hereafter the two methods of translation just described will be referred to as simply the *mechanical translation* and/or *literal translation* and the *conceptual translation* and/or *conceptual hypothesis* respectively. It is a misrepresentation for advocates of the *conceptual translation* to assert that the *mechanical translation* does not account for Smith's role as translator; nothing could be more misleading, for the term *mechanical* only has reference to how Smith's seer stone was said to operate, and does not preclude the fact that Joseph Smith had to be spiritually in tune for the stone to work. Thus, David Whitmer, in describing the *mechanical* manner in which the stone delivered the translation, also mentioned that Joseph Smith had to be in the right frame of mind before the stone would give the translation to him. David Whitmer, *An Address to All Believers in Christ* (Richmond, Mo.: 1887), p. 30.

hypothesis must be viewed as an apologetic device which is contradicted by historical evidence. Next, it will be shown that because the anachronistic errors in the *Book of Mormon* are more complex than Ashment is willing to admit, the so-called *conceptual hypothesis* does not satisfactorily explain the *Book of Mormon's* historical blunders. Given the above two points, and Ashment's own acknowledgment that the *Book of Mormon* is written in Joseph Smith's own style,[4] it is hardly possible to view the *Book of Mormon* as anything but nineteenth-century fiction, its author and hoaxer being Joseph Smith.

Early Testimony Regarding Method of Translation: The Theological Problem

Ashment argues that Joseph Smith never gave us a clear statement on how he "translated" the *Book of Mormon,* and that we are therefore left to speculate on the matter. However, Joseph did say on one occasion that the title page of the *Book of Mormon* is a *"literal* translation,"[5] but Ashment assures us that Joseph Smith did not mean "literal" in the normal sense of the word. What Joseph really meant, according to Ashment, was that the ideas on the plates flowed into his mind and that those ideas were then expressed in the best English at his command, thus producing "a *literal* rendering of the 'subject matter' which he perceived." However, the content of Joseph Smith's statement implies the *normal translation method,*

---

4. On the syntax and style of the *Book of Mormon,* Egyptologist Ashment states:

It has been instructive to compare the Book of Mormon with ancient Egyptian and Hebrew texts in an effort to ascertain if their syntax and style match the very distinctive syntax and style of the Book of Mormon: incomplete sentences, an abnormally frequent use of circumstantial gerund phrases, numerous digressions which often develop into a chain of digressions before returning to the main text, and an extensive use of adverbs and conjunctions which frequently incorrectly function to draw relationships where none are possible according to context.

Ancient Egyptian or Semitic texts known to this writer do not display those characteristics. Instead, they tend to be "tightly" structured and concise (a necessary prerequisite for a period of time in which writing materials were scarce and very expensive). Incomplete sentences are not characteristic (except in lacunae) nor is a high frequency of circumstantials. Numerous digressions of the type in the Book of Mormon do not occur, and the adverbs and conjuctives [*sic*] are used with a specific syntactic pattern intended. On the other hand, the salient characteristics of the syntax and style of the Book of Mormon also tend to be the prominent features of the other literary efforts of the prophet—viz., the 1832 history which he wrote and dictated, the Doctrine and Covenants, and the Pearl of Great Price.

5. B. H. Roberts, ed., *History of the Church of Jesus Christ of Latter-day Saints,* 7 vols., 2nd ed. rev. (Salt Lake City: Deseret Book Co., 1969), I:71. (Hereafter cited as DHC Documentary History of the Church.) Cf., *Times and Seasons* (October 15, 1842), III:943. Emphasis in quotations throughout this article is mine unless otherwise indicated.

which gives consideration to the words on the plates rather than rendering into English mere concepts flowing into the mind. Thus Joseph Smith was particular enough to mention in his statement that the *"genuine* and *literal* translation"* of the script *"as* recorded on the plates ran from right to left, "the language of the whole running the same as all Hebrew writing in general."[6]

Further, Ashment attempts to redefine and broaden the meaning of the term "translation" as it is used in connection with the *Book of Mormon.* While it is true that Joseph Smith sometimes used the word "translation" to refer to something other than the carrying over of one language into another, these other uses should not confuse us when he is clearly using the term in the more restricted sense. For example, Ashment compares the "translation" of the *Book of Mormon* with the "translation" of Joseph Smith's *Inspired Revision* of the Bible. The two processes should never be confused as Ashment has done. In the first instance, "translation" was a rendering of one language into another from records Joseph Smith claimed to possess, whereas, in the second instance, "translation" did not involve any records or original manuscripts, and hence was not a carrying over from one language into another; rather, "translation" here means to "express in different words, rephrase, or paraphrase in explanation."[7] The term "translation," therefore, can be legitimately used to describe both processes although they were very different things.

Testimony regarding the method used by Joseph Smith to translate the *Book of Mormon* is much more substantial than Ashment is willing to admit. Those few Mormons who still believe the *Book of Mormon* is the product of *mechanical* and *literal translation* find it difficult to ignore the statements given by David Whitmer and Martin Harris,[8] both of whom were present when Smith translated the *Book of Mormon.* According to the testimony of Martin Harris, who acted as scribe for Joseph Smith,

---

6. Ibid. Joseph Smith's statement here, however, is in direct conflict with a newly found document. The document is a facsimile of characters said to have been copied from the *Book of Mormon* plates by Smith in 1828. In this document the characters are placed in columns, and were apparently meant to be read from left to right. See Danel W. Bachman, "Sealed in a Book: Preliminary Observations on the Newly Found 'Anthon Transcript,' " *Brigham Young University Studies* 20 (Spring 1980):321-45.

7. Robert J. Matthews, *"A Plainer Translation": Joseph Smith's Translation of the Bible, A History and Commentary* (Provo, Utah: Brigham Young University Press, 1975), p. 13.

8. Evidently these Mormons are unaware of the problems connected with the acceptance of the *mechanical translation.* Ashment himself tries to warn his fellow Mormons of the dangers of such a position. "In this naive view," says Ashment, "Joseph Smith could be nothing but a fallen prophet, having altered a divinely-received text."

by the aid of the seer stone, sentences would appear and were read by the Prophet and written by Martin, and when finished he would say, "Written," and if correctly written, that sentence would disappear and another appear in its place, but if not written correctly it remained until corrected, so that the translation was just as it was engraved on the plates, precisely in the language then used.[9]

This same testimony is borne out by David Whitmer.

I will now give you a description of the manner in which the Book of Mormon was translated. Joseph Smith would put the seer stone into a hat, and put his face in the hat, drawing it closely around his face to exclude the light; and in the darkness the spiritual light would shine. A piece of something resembling parchment would appear, and on that appeared the writing. One character at a time would appear, and under it was the interpretation in English. Brother Joseph would read off the English to Oliver Cowdery, who was his principle scribe, and when it was written down and repeated to Brother Joseph to see if it was correct, then it would disappear, and another character with the interpretation would appear. Thus the Book of Mormon was translated by the gift and power of God, and not by any power of man.[10]

If the descriptions given by Harris and Whitmer are accurate, says Ashment, then "the resultant translation would have been a mere mechanical recitation of divine words which appeared in the seer stone." While Ashment does not want to say that Harris and Whitmer invented their descriptions (for to do so would bring their special testimony of the *Book of Mormon* into question), he does say the descriptions are "so far removed from the event," and hence "they stand a good chance of not accurately reflecting what actually transpired." Although this suggestion does not account for the remarkable agreement in the two descriptions,[11] there are still other sources to consider before accusing Messrs. Harris and Whitmer of bad memories. According to Father John A. Clark, who spoke with Harris during the time he was acting as Smith's scribe, Harris told him Smith looked "through his spectacles . . . and would then write down or repeat what he saw, which, when repeated aloud, was written down by Harris."[12]

9. Reported by Edward Stevenson in *Deseret Evening News* (September 5, 1870).

10. Whitmer, op. cit., p. 12.

11. Ashment agrees, but offers no explanation as to why the Harris/Whitmer descriptions are so similar. He states: "David Whitmer's declaration and the *almost identical* one produced by Martin Harris imply that absolutely no textual changes were possible in the Book of Mormon, for such revisions would reflect the word of man, not inspiration from God." Such differences which do occur between the two witnesses' statements are of such minor importance that they should not detract from the major thrust of their descriptions.

12. *Gleanings By the Way* (Philadelphia: W. J. & J. K. Simon, 1842), p. 230.

And as early as 1834 anti-Mormon writer Eber D. Howe wrote about the "various verbal accounts . . . which were given out by the Smith family," which included a description of the manner of translating the *Book of Mormon*.

> . . . the Lord showed and communicated to him every word and letter of the Book. Instead of looking at the characters inscribed upon the plates, the prophet was obliged to resort to the old "peep stone," which he formerly used in money-digging.[13] This he placed in a hat, or box, into which he also thrust his face. Through the stone he could then discover a single word at a time, which he repeated aloud to his amanuensis, who committed it to paper, when another word would immediately appear, and thus the performance continued to the end of the book.[14]

Joseph Knight, who became Joseph Smith's friend during the translation period, described the translation process sometime before his death in 1847 as follows:

> Now the way he translated was he put the urim and thummim into his hat and Darkned his Eyes then he would take a sentence and it would appear in Brite Roman Letters. Then he would tell the writer and he would write it. Then that would go away the next sentence would Come and so on. But if it was not Spelt rite it would not go away till it was rite, so we see it was marvelous.[15]

Because of the remarkable agreement in the descriptions of Harris and Whitmer together with other early accounts, it is no longer possible to accuse the two men of faulty memories. It is, therefore, not proper to view the Harris/Whitmer accounts as misstatements made in later life; rather, they are descriptions which originated right from the very birth of Mormonism. The most likely explanation for the striking similarity in the Harris/Whitmer accounts is that the descriptions originate with Joseph Smith himself. In fact, that is exactly what Whitmer, Harris and others claimed. According to Whitmer, Joseph Smith translated the *Book of Mormon*

by means of one dark colored, opaque stone, called a "Seer Stone,"

---

13. For Joseph Smith's use of a "peep stone" in hunting for buried treasure before he began "translating" the *Book of Mormon,* see Wesley P. Walters, "Joseph Smith's Bainbridge, N.Y., Court Trials," *Westminster Theological Journal* 36, 2 (Winter 1974):123-55. And for the occultic connection of Joseph Smith's use of the "peep stone," see Walters, "From Occult to Cult with Joseph Smith, Jr.," *The Journal of Pastoral Practice* 1, 2 (Summer 1977):121-37.

14. *Mormonism Unvailed* [sic] (Painesville, Ohio, 1834), p. 18.

15. Spelling and capitalization as in original, as quoted in Dean Jessee, "Joseph Knight's Recollection of Early Mormon History," *Brigham Young University Studies* 17 (Autumn 1976):35.

which was placed in the crown of a hat, into which Joseph put his face, so as to exclude the external light. Then, a spiritual light would shine forth, and parchment would appear before Joseph, upon which was a line of characters from the plates, and under it, the translation in English; *at least, so Joseph said.*[16]

The Rochester *Advertiser and Telegraph* (August 31, 1829) and the *Rochester Gem* (September 5, 1829) contain information evidently from Martin Harris dealing with the translation of the *Book of Mormon*. The *Rochester Advertiser and Telegraph* has the following:

> By placing the spectacles in a hat, and looking into it, Smith could (*he said so at least*) interpret these characters.[17]

And Pomeroy Tucker, who helped read the proofs for the *Book of Mormon*, wrote:

> The manuscripts were in the handwriting of one Oliver Cowdery, which had been written down by him, *as he and Smith declared*, from the translations, *word for word*, as made by the latter with aid of the mammoth spectacles or Urim and Thummim.[18]

Matthew L. Davis, a Washington correspondent for the *New York Enquirer*, wrote a letter to his wife and accurately described many of Smith's teachings. Davis acquired his knowledge of Joseph Smith's teachings from a speech he heard Smith deliver in Washington. The next day, February 6, 1840, Davis wrote:

> The Mormon Bible, he said, was communicated to him, *direct from heaven*. If there was such a thing on earth, as the author of it, then he (Smith) was the author; *but the idea that he wished to impress was, that he had penned it as dictated by God.*[19]

The mechanical method of translating the *Book of Mormon*, as described

---

16. *Saints' Herald* 26 (November 15, 1879):341.

17. As quoted in Francis W. Kirkham, *A New Witness for Christ in America*, 2 vols. (Salt Lake City: Utah Printing Co., 1959), II:31-32.

18. Pomeroy Tucker, *Origin, Rise, and Progress of Mormonism* (New York: D. Appleton and Co., 1867), p. 36. John H. Gilbert, Tucker's fellow worker in the printing shop, recalled that Martin Harris told him that "the spectacles turned the hyroglyphics into good English." "Memorandum, made by John H. Gilbert, Esq., Sept. 8th, 1892, Palmyra, N.Y.," as published in Wilford C. Wood, *Joseph Smith Begins His Work*, 2 vols. (Salt Lake City, 1958), I.

19. DHC IV:79. Emphasis mine except for the words *"direct from heaven."* Although the original source for the Davis report is presently unavailable, the letter was probably printed somewhere in the missing numbers of the *New York Enquirer*. See Andrew F. Ehat and Lyndon W. Cook, *The Words of Joseph Smith*, The Religious Studies Monograph Series, vol. 6 (Provo, Utah: Brigham Young University, 1980), p. 46.

by Harris and Whitmer, can be further substantiated by Joseph Smith himself. It may not be entirely correct, therefore, for Ashment to say Joseph Smith never left us a clear statement on how he translated the *Book of Mormon*. In the course of translating, 116 pages of the manuscript were stolen from Smith, who explained in his Preface to the first edition of the *Book of Mormon* why he did not retranslate the lost portion.

> . . . I translated, by the gift and power of God, and caused to be written, one hundred and sixteen pages, the which I took from the Book of Lehi, which was an account abridged from the plates of Lehi, by the hand of Mormon; which said account, some person or persons have stolen and kept from me, notwithstanding my utmost exertions to recover it again—and being commanded of the Lord that I should not translate the same over again, for Satan had put it into their hearts to tempt the Lord their God, *by altering the words,* that they did read contrary from that which I translated and caused to be written; and if I should bring forth *the same words* again, or, in otherwords, if I should translate the same over again, they would publish that which they had stolen, and Satan would stir up the hearts of this generation, that they might not receive this work. . . .[20]

Clearly, the implication here is that if Joseph Smith had retranslated the lost 116 pages, or "brought forth the same words again," the only difference between the two documents would have been at the places where his enemies had "altered" the words. This statement by Joseph Smith is as strong an indication that he considered the *Book of Mormon* a product of *mechanical* and *literal translation* as one could possibly hope for. Furthermore, the loss of the 116 pages also has some other interesting ramifications which reflect on Joseph Smith's "gift" of translation. Arthur Budvarson observed that the loss of the 116 pages

> afforded a remarkable opportunity for Joseph Smith to have proven to the world that the work was true. All he needed to do was to reproduce an exact copy of the stolen pages, then perhaps even the thieves would have been converted! (The stolen pages were written in longhand and any alterations could have been easily detected.)
>
> But Joseph had failed to make a copy of his writings, so it was not possible for him to make an exact duplicate. In order to get around this, he says that God commanded him that he "should not translate the same over again. . . ."

20. Preface to the first edition of the *Book of Mormon* (Palmyra, N. Y.: E. B. Grandin, 1830). This Preface was subsequently removed from later editions of the *Book of Mormon*. Cf. D&C 10, esp. verse 31.

This one incident alone . . . furnishes positive proof that the Book of Mormon is not a God-given, angel-protected book![21]

Mormon scholar Sidney B. Sperry, who attempted to answer Mr. Budvarson's charges, said that since the *Book of Mormon* was conceptually translated, it would have been impossible for Joseph Smith to reproduce the exact wording of the 116-page manuscript.[22] But Mr. Sperry seems to have missed the whole point of Smith's Preface, which indicates that Smith could "bring forth the same words again," but that if he did his enemies would alter the words in the stolen manuscript so that they would "read contrary" from that which he had translated. Thus Joseph Smith places blame for any variant readings squarely on the shoulders of his enemies.

It is unfortunate for Ashment that his only reference to contemporary testimony is not only thirdhand information but upon closer examination does not even support his translation hypothesis. Instead of quoting his source directly, Ashment chose to quote another historian's interpretation of the source. Ashment quotes D. Michael Quinn, who is giving an editorial comment on a letter written in German by Rev. Diedrich Willers (June 18, 1830), as saying that this contemporary account implies that the translation of the *Book of Mormon* was "a product of spiritual impressions to Joseph Smith rather than an automatic appearance of the English words." The actual source, however, though vague as it is, cannot be used to support the *conceptual hypothesis*. Although Willers mentions the "spectacles, without which he could not translate these plates, that by using these spectacles, he (Smith) would be in a position to read these ancient languages, which he had never studied," he does not seem very clear as to how the spectacles could actually help in the translation process. But however the "spectacles" worked, Willers still correctly understood the "translation" was a product of direct divine communication, that *"the Holy Ghost would reveal to him the translation in the English language."*[23] The theological problem remains so long as it is claimed the Spirit of God revealed to Smith the translation *in* English. Thus even Rev. Willers' account must be added to the large body of testimony that converges on the central theme that the *Book of Mormon* was originally claimed to be the product of direct, God-given translation.

21. *The Book of Mormon Examined* (La Mesa, Calif., 1959), pp. 13-14.

22. *Problems of the Book of Mormon* (Salt Lake City: Bookcraft Publishers, 1967), p. 196 (subsequently published as *Answers to Book of Mormon Questions*).

23. D. Michael Quinn, "The First Months of Mormonism: A Contemporary View by Rev. Diedrich Willers," *New York History* 54 (July 1973):326.

Ashment and his fellow advocates of the *conceptual hypothesis* like to refer to *Doctrine and Covenants* section 9 for the "Lord's description of the translation process." After Oliver Cowdery had failed in his attempt at translation, Joseph Smith produced a revelation which "excused" Cowdery's failure.

> Behold, you have not understood; you have supposed that I would give it unto you, when you took no thought save it was to ask me. But, behold, I say unto you, that *you must study it out in your mind;* then you must ask me if it be right, and if it is right I will cause that your bosom shall burn within you; therefore, you shall feel that it is right. But if it be not right you shall have no such feelings, but you shall have a stupor of thought that shall cause you to forget the thing which is wrong; therefore, you cannot write that which is sacred save it be given you from me. Now, if you had known this you could have translated. . . .[24]

This is not, to be sure, a description of how Joseph Smith translated, but rather of how Oliver Cowdery *could have* translated. There is, however, ample evidence that the above revelation is not an accurate description of how Joseph Smith translated the *Book of Mormon*. First, how could Joseph Smith (or Oliver Cowdery, for that matter) be expected to know enough

---

24. D&C 9:7-10. There are two common assumption which are sometimes made when reading the text of section 9. The first assumption is that Cowdery attempted to translate the *Book of Mormon* plates. When Cowdery was promised the gift of translation, he was told that "there are records which contain much of my gospel, which have been kept back because of the wickedness of the people . . . you [shall] assist in bringing to light, with your gift, those parts of my scriptures which have been hidden because of iniquity" (D&C 6:26, 27). And again, "you shall receive a knowledge concerning the engravings of old records, which are ancient, which contain those parts of my scripture . . . you may translate and receive knowledge from all those ancient records which have been hid up, that are sacred" (8:1, 11). But because Cowdery had failed to translate, the Lord told him to wait until the *Book of Mormon* is finished before starting work on the "other records" (9:2). It is not clear what records besides the *Book of Mormon* Cowdery tried to translate, but it is interesting that the *Book of Mormon* itself mentions other Nephite records (cf. Alma 37:1-4; Hel. 3:15, 16; 4 Ne. 48, 49; Morm. 1:3, 4).

The second assumption is that Cowdery used either the Urim and Thummim or the seer stone. Nowhere are we told that Cowdery used either of these instruments. *Doctrines and Covenants* Section 8, as it first appeared in the *Book of Commandments* (chap. VII), told Cowdery that he had both the "gift" of revelation ("I will tell you in your mind and in your heart by the Holy Ghost") and the "gift of working with the rod" ("the rod of nature . . . whatsoever you shall ask me to tell you by that means, that will I grant unto you, that you shall know"). Cowdery, with his divining rod and the spirit of revelation, is instructed by the Lord to "ask that you may know the mysteries of God, and that you may translate all those ancient records. . . ." If Cowdery used either or both these "gifts," being unlike Joseph Smith's seer stone (i.e., non-visual), it may very well explain why both sections 8 and 9 put stress on the mind and heart. This explanation would make Cowdery's method of translation (as it is described in sections 8 and 9) vastly different than the method used by Joseph Smith to translate the *Book of Mormon*. In addition, this interpretation has the advantage of removing the apparent contradiction between the accounts of the eyewitnesses and the description of translation in sections 8 and 9.

about "Reformed" Egyptian to "study it out" in the mind? Second, the testimony of eyewitnesses states that there was no hesitation during the translation process. And third, the process of studying it out in the mind, then seeking divine approval, and if wrong starting all over, would have occupied much more time than is usually assigned for the translation of the *Book of Mormon*.[25] Mormon writer George Reynolds made this observation long ago when he wrote:

> Objection has been made to the divinity of the Book of Mormon on the ground that the account given in the publications of the Church, of the time occupied in the work of translation is far too short for the accomplishment of such a labor. . . . But at the outset it must be recollected that the translation was accomplished by no common method, by no ordinary means. It was done by divine aid. There were no delays over obscure passages, no difficulties over the choice of words, no stoppages from ignorance of the translator; no time was wasted in investigation or argument over the value, intent or meaning of certain characters, and there were no references to authorities. These difficulties to human work were removed. The translation was as simple as when a clerk writes from dictation. The translation of the characters appeared on the Urim and Thummim, sentence by sentence, and as soon as one was correctly transcribed the next would appear. So the enquiry narrows down to the consideration of this simple question, how much could Oliver Cowdery write in a day? . . .[26]

Because of the obvious problems with accepting *Doctrine and Covenants* section 9 as a legitimate description of how Joseph Smith translated the *Book of Mormon,* plus the fact that it contradicts the historical evidence we have discussed for the *mechanical translation,* some students of the subject have come to regard the words to Cowdery as a "revelation" of convenience which was used to excuse Cowdery's failure, much like the "revelation"

---

25. Seventy-five days are usually assigned for the time occupied in translating the *Book of Mormon* (see Kirkham, op. cit., I:208-27). Writing in longhand from dictation is a very time-consuming procedure, especially if the scribe is made to repeat every sentence as it is written down. But even this time schedule becomes crowded when it is claimed that Joseph Smith, in addition to translating the *Book of Mormon,* also dictated at least ten revelations, debated neighbors, and received visits from heavenly messengers (DHC I:31-71). Although they were at times able to translate uninterrupted (DHC I:44), that was not always the case (DHC I:59). Taking all this into consideration, it is surprising that Oliver Cowdery was able to write by dictation an average of 3550 words per day. See Robert N. Hullinger, *Mormon Answer to Skepticism, Why Joseph Smith Wrote the Book of Mormon* (St. Louis: Clayton Publishing House, 1980), p. 16. At such a pace there could not have been much struggle over the translation.

26. *The Myth of the "Manuscript Found"* (Salt Lake City: Juvenile Instructor Office, 1883), p. 71. See also N. L. Nelson, *The Mormon Point of View* (Provo, Utah, 1904), pp. 124-25.

which conveniently excused Smith from retranslating the stolen 116-page manuscript.[27]

Even if Ashment were to insist upon using *Doctrine and Covenants* section 9, it must still be admitted that the original manuscript of the *Book of Mormon* has God's sanction on *every* word, for every word not "given you from me" would have been quickly forgotten with a "stupor of thought." Furthermore, since the revelation places the words with God, not the translator ("you cannot write that which is *sacred* save it be *given you from me*"), the theological problem remains in force. Thus no matter which way one turns, one is confronted with the dilemma of Joseph Smith tampering with a "sacred" text, for he freely added to and altered the text in over 3,000 places in subsequent editions. Moreover, God's sanction would be on the bad grammar and anachronisms. Therefore, section 9 does not even harmonize with Ashment's translation hypothesis. This may very well have been the reason why Ashment chose not to discuss this revelation in detail. Certainly it was not to his advantage to do so.

Finally, Ashment's suggestion that if Smith had considered the *Book of Mormon* text inviolate, then he certainly would never have revised it, must be rejected on the ground that the true nature of the changes was not openly stated. In fact, readers of the second edition of the *Book of Mormon* had the impression that the only changes made in the text were the correction of "typographical errors which always occur in manuscript editions," so the new edition read closer to the divinely given, original text.[28] But only those with access to the original manuscript would know the exact nature of the changes, that Smith had freely added to and altered the "sacred" text in over 3,000 places.[29] Certainly it would have been contradictory for Smith openly

---

27. E.g., Sandra Tanner, personal letter to this writer, November 13, 1978. Notice the shift from D&C 8:1-2 (". . . ask in faith . . . believing that you shall receive . . . I will tell you in your mind. . . .") to D&C 9:7-8 (". . . you have supposed that I would give it unto you, when you took no thought save it was to ask me . . . you must study it out in your mind . . . .").

28. The Preface to the second edition of the *Book of Mormon,* which was removed from subsequent editions, reads in part as follows:

> Individuals acquainted with book printing, are aware of the numerous typographical errors which always occur in manuscript editions. It is only necessary to say, that the whole has been carefully re-examined and compared with the original manuscripts, by elder Joseph Smith, Jr. the translator of the book of Mormon, assisted by the present printer, brother O. Cowdery, who formerly wrote the greatest portion of the same as dictated by brother Joseph. (Kirtland, Ohio, 1837)

29. Richard P. Howard, *Restoration Scriptures: A Study of Their Textual Development* (Independence, Mo.: Herald House, 1969), p. 41. Stan Larson, "A Study of Some Textual

to make changes in the *Book of Mormon* while at the same time claiming the "translation" came directly from God. It would be expected, therefore, that Joseph Smith would not only try to hide the true nature of his changes but also to be protective of the original manuscript. It is reported that an apostate had stolen the manuscript from Smith, and that he had to resort to "stratagem" to regain possession of it again.[30] The fear of the possibility of the original manuscript being used against his claims of *mechanical translation* may explain why Smith seemed anxious to deposit the manuscript in a safe place. On October 2, 1841, Warren Foote was standing near the southeast cornerstone of the Nauvoo House (which was then being constructed), when Joseph Smith walked up to place the original *Book of Mormon* manuscript in the cornerstone. After Joseph had made sure all the pages of the manuscript were there,[31] according to Foote, Joseph said "he wanted to put that in there, as he had trouble enough with it."[32]

The original *Book of Mormon* manuscript was subsequently removed from the cornerstone in the 1880's, and today it continues to cause *trouble* for Joseph Smith and his claims about the *Book of Mormon*.

Variations in the Book of Mormon Comparing the Original and the Printer's Manuscripts and the 1830, the 1837 and the 1840 Editions," Master's thesis, Brigham Young University, April 1974.

30. Hyrum Smith is reported as saying the original manuscript "once fell into the hands of an apostate (I [Hyrum] think one of the Whitmers) and they had to resort to stratagem to get possession of it again" (letter from John Brown to John Taylor, December 20, 1879, as quoted in Dean Jessee, "The Original Book of Mormon Manuscript," *Brigham Young University Studies* 10 [Spring 1970]:264). The fact that there were two manuscript copies of the *Book of Mormon* does not detract from the importance of the original, dictated manuscript since only the dictated manuscript had God's sanction on every word (D&C 9:7-9; 17:6; DHC I:55). The existence of the printer's copy would not have caused Smith much concern since it carried no divine sanction and was not prepared with divine instrumentality. If the printer's copy would have been used against Smith's claims of inspiration, he could have easily explained that he had restored the 1837 text to read like the dictated manuscript and that any differences the printer's copy had were due to the scribe misreading the God-given, dictated manuscript. Indeed, Cowdery had misread the dictated manuscript in a number of places when preparing the printer's copy (see Larson, op. cit., pp. 234-83). As long as the original dictated manuscript remained in his possession, Smith's integrity as a prophet inspired by God to translate the *Book of Mormon* was safe.

31. Ebinezer Robinson, who was present when Smith placed the manuscript in the cornerstone, reported that before he did so, he said: "I will examine to see if it is all here. . ." (*The Return*, II:314-15, as quoted in Jessee, op. cit., p. 264).

32. Warren Foote, "Dairy [*sic*]," October 2, 1841, vol. 1, p. 57, as quoted in Jessee, op. cit., p. 264. Seventy-two surviving sheets (144 pages) of the original *Book of Mormon* manuscript are now housed in Library-Archives of the Historical Department of the Church of Jesus Christ of Latter-day Saints, Salt Lake City, Utah.

Anachronistic Errors in the Book of Mormon:
The Historical Problem

In a footnote Ashment gives reference to a very valuable article written by H. Michael Marquardt, ''The Use of the Bible in the Book of Mormon.'' This article from *The Journal of Pastoral Practice* discusses the *Book of Mormon's* strange use of New Testament quotations and phrases in its Old Testament portion (a list of 200 examples is given). When the *mechanical* and *literal translation* method is taken into account, then each of Marquardt's examples takes on added significance as unexplainable anachronisms—historical blunders which demonstrate the *Book of Mormon's* modern origin. The following examples are taken from Marquardt's article:

Book of Mormon (supposedly written prior to 70 B.C. and ''translated'' c. A.D. 1830)	*New Testament* (written after A.D. 30 and published A.D. 1611)
1. and there shall be one fold and one shepherd (1 Nephi 22:25).	and there shall be one fold, and one shepherd (John 10:16).
2. in the mansions of my Father (Enos 27).	In my Father's house are many mansions (John 14:2).
3. If they be good, to the resurrection of endless life and happiness; and if they be evil, to the resurrection of endless damnation (Mosiah 16:11).	they that have done good, unto the resurrection of life, and they that have done evil, unto the resurrection of damnation (John 5:29).
4. one faith and one baptism (Mosiah 18:21).	one faith, one baptism (Eph. 4:5)
5. the Spirit is the same yesterday, today and forever (2 Nephi 2:4).	Jesus Christ the same yesterday and today, and forever (Heb. 13:8).

Ashment, however, attempts to use the *conceptual hypothesis* to explain away the problem with the *Book of Mormon's* use of New Testament phraseology in its Old Testament time period. Ashment's argument runs as follows:

> Certainly one of the best ways to account for the hundreds of New Testament phrases which occur in the Old Testament portions of the Book of Mormon lies in a realization of the prophet's intimate familiarity with biblical terminology from his early home environment. Thus, when translating what to him was to be regarded as sacred scripture, it would only be natural to use the scriptural language with which he would be most familiar—King James English. . . . Otherwise it must

be assumed that the Nephites somehow were privy to the exact same figures of speech that would not develop in the Old World until New Testament times.

Actually, Ashment is understating the problem with the *Book of Mormon's* use of the biblical material. Marquardt, however, points out that while Mormons will try to use the *conceptual hypothesis* to escape the anachronistic evidence against the *Book of Mormon,* such a hypothesis ignores the fact that the *Book of Mormon's* "use of the Bible goes far deeper than mere use of phrases from the New Testament in the Old Testament period," but also its author at times "reflects upon and expands on the New Testament *interpretation* of Old Testament material and allows his imagination to create Old Testament events that flow from this New Testament interpretation." Marquardt then gives Alma, chapters 12 and 13, as an example of this procedure.

> Hebrews employs Genesis 14:18-20 together with Psalm 2:7 and 110:4 to establish that the Messiah holds a priesthood higher than that of the Levitical priesthood, and that this priesthood "after the order of Melchisedec" has superseded and abolished the Levitical one (Heb. 5:5-10; 6:20; 7:1-12). The author of the *Book of Mormon* builds upon this New Testament interpretation and adds his own misinterpretation of this material to create an entire order of priests "after the order of the Son" (Alma 13:9), "being a type of his order" (13:6), of whom Melchisedec is but the leading example (13:9). Furthermore, Hebrews' interpretation of Melchisedec's name and title (King of righteousness . . . King of peace") is expanded into an imaginary historical situation in which Melchisedec successfully calls his people to repentance and thus to righteousness and peace. This material is then worked together into a somewhat systematic doctrinal exposition which utilizes other New Testament phrases from such sources as the Gospels, I Corinthians, and Revelation.[33]

Because of such evidence from the *Book of Mormon,* Marquardt concludes that "the New Testament quotations become a part of the very fabric of the text and cannot be regarded as mere figures of speech employed in the process of 'translating' the *Book of Mormon.*"[34] Thus, even if we were to ignore the early testimony regarding the method of translation and allow Ashment his hypothesis, it still would not be possible for him to explain the historical problem the *Book of Mormon* creates when it borrows from the New Testament. While Ashment's translation hypothesis may appeal to the

33. H. Michael Marquardt, "The Use of the Bible in the Book of Mormon," *The Journal of Pastoral Practice* 2, 2 (1978):98-99.

34. Ibid.

uncritical reader who has been led by Mormon apologists to believe the *Book of Mormon's* use of the biblical material is limited to similar terminology, such a hypothesis is wholly unsatisfactory to the more careful reader who is aware that the *Book of Mormon's* use of the Bible goes far deeper than the mere borrowing of simple terminology, but rather, as Marquardt has shown, it actually "reflects upon and expands on the New Testament *interpretation* of Old Testament material."

The *Book of Mormon's* use of the biblical material is further complicated when its author blunders by accidentally quoting Peter instead of Moses. In 1 Nephi 22:20, Nephi (c. 600 B.C.) should have quoted the "words of Moses" in Deuteronomy 18:15, 18-19, but instead quotes Peter's paraphrase of Moses' words in Acts 3:22-23. Interestingly, this same blunder is repeated in 3 Nephi 20:23-26, where the risen Christ should have quoted to the Nephites the words which "Moses spake" in Deuteronomy, but instead not only quotes Peter's paraphrase but also quotes the apostle's own words from the book of Acts. The same situation occurs when the *Book of Mormon* author quotes the words of Malachi (4:1) in 1 Nephi 22:15 over a hundred years before Malachi wrote them. Examples could be multiplied, but space does not permit it; the serious student, however, is referred to Marquardt's excellent article for a more thorough treatment.

Conclusion

Because Ashment has failed to prove his translation hypothesis, and the evidence clearly supports the descriptions of Harris and Whitmer, all the problems he attempted to answer with his hypothesis must fall back into his own lap. It is he, therefore, who has shown most clearly that Joseph Smith's claims about the *Book of Mormon* cannot be true. There can be no other explanation for the *Book of Mormon's* use of the New Testament in its Old Testament period than the *Book of Mormon* being a modern composition, its author having access to the King James Bible. The presence of bad grammar, redundancies, and chronological errors are evidences that the *Book of Mormon* is from human origin rather than a God-given "translation" as Joseph Smith and his associates claimed.[35] Further, that changes were made in the "sacred" text may indicate to some Mormons that Joseph Smith was a fallen prophet, but it may also indicate that Smith recognized that such

---

35. The obvious chronological problem with the reading in Mosiah 21:28 and Ether 4:1 resulted in the change of "Benjamin" to "Mosiah." For a discussion of this problem, see Stan Larson, "Early Book of Mormon Texts," *Sunstone* 1, 4 (Fall 1976):47.

mistakes were evidence against his story about the God-given translation, so he corrected them under the guise of printer's errors. These are conclusions which Mormon apologists like Ashment want to avoid at any cost—even if it means advancing a new translation hypothesis which is unsupported by the evidence.

The presence of anachronisms, however, is a sure indication of the *Book of Mormon's* modern production. The *Book of Mormon* cannot, therefore, be regarded as a *translation* of an ancient document. Thus a more meaningful and fruitful examination of the *Book of Mormon's* contents will result from the view that it is a nineteenth-century religious fictional book.[36]

---

36. For an excellent example of a study based on the interpretation that the *Book of Mormon* is nineteenth-century religious fiction, see Marquardt, ''Early Nineteenth Century Events Reflected in the Book of Mormon, *The Journal of Pastoral Practice* 3, 1 (1979):114-36.

THE STRAW MEN OF THE WATCHTOWER SOCIETY

M. KURT GOEDELMAN

The dictionary gives as one meaning of "straw man": "an unimportant person, object or discussion," and illustrates the usage with a sentence which says: "your argument is a straw man intended to divert us from the real issues" (*Random House Dictionary*).

The Watchtower Society, in its attempt to deny the deity of Christ, has put forth just such straw men. These are parts of biblical verses intended to divert us from the real issue of Christ's deity, stated so clearly and repeatedly throughout the Bible. They are relatively "unimportant" phrases, selected and distorted by the Witness leaders, which are elevated to positions of prominence in the discussion of Jesus' Godhood. They are straw men and, like straw men, cannot stand up under the assault of truth and careful examination of the biblical text. Presented here are some of these distorted passages along with the biblical truth that blows them away.

STRAW MAN #1

Revelation 3:14—"The Beginning of God's Creation"

The Jehovah's Witnesses here announce that the Lord Jesus Christ is a creature, being the first one created or "the beginning of God's creation." In the original Greek language the word John used for "beginning" is *arche*. *We derive our word architect* from this Greek word. When speaking of philosophical matters, such as the creation of the universe, *arche* was used as a technical term meaning "first cause," "origin," "source." Aelius Aristides (*c*. A.D. 175), for example, wrote, "Zeus is *the first cause (arche)* of all things and every thing is from God." This clearly does not mean Zeus was the first creature made, but rather he was the creator of all things. Again, the Jewish writer Josephus (a contemporary of the author of the Book of Revelation), in a work combatting the Greek anti-Semitism of his day,

92

wrote, "The universe is in God's hands. . . . He is the beginning (first cause, *arche*), the middle, and the end of all things" (*Against Apion* II, 190). Josephus, by these words, is certainly not suggesting that God was the first creature to be made. Similarly, in speaking of Jesus as "the beginning (*arche*) of God's creation," the text is proclaiming that Jesus (the faithful and true witness) is the source, origin or architect of God's creation, and *not* merely the first creature made by God.

STRAW MAN #2

Colossians 1:15—"The First-born of All Creation"

The Watchtower Society here again asserts that our Lord Jesus was the first created being by a misunderstanding of this phrase, "the first-born of all creation." Much emphasis is placed by the Witnesses on the term "first-born." However, they distort the biblical usage of the term and twist the meaning to support their position. To claim that Jesus was created (first created) because he is announced as the "first-born" is an erroneous conclusion. If the apostle Paul had wished to express the view that Christ was created, he could have done so by using the Greek word *protoktistos* (first created), but the word he used was *prototokos* (first-born). *Prototokos* (first-born) is the one who became heir to the family estate. It also denotes preeminence or first in rank. A few examples of the usage of the term "first-born" makes this biblical meaning clear. Jehovah (Yahweh) tells us in Psalm 89:27 that He will make David his "first-born." The Greek translation of the Old Testament (*c.* 200 B.C.) here uses the same word, *prototokos,* even though David was actually the youngest of all the sons of Jesse and not literally his first-born (I Sam. 16:1-13). Further, in Scripture there are at least two other cases of this "first-born" rank or heirship being conferred upon the younger sons. In verse 52 of Genesis 41, Ephraim is presented as the second child born to Joseph, yet in Jeremiah 31:9 God calls Ephraim his "first-born," and the Greek translation again uses *prototokos* (Jer. 38:9 in the Greek version). Again, in Genesis 25:29ff., we see the "first-born" rank transferred as the lives of Esau and Jacob are unfolded. Here Esau sells to Jacob his first-born heirship for bread and pottage of lentils.

The Watchtower position is shown further to be a misunderstanding by the verses following verse 15, their pet text. Paul states concerning Christ that *all things* were created by Him, and He obviously did not create Himself (see Isa. 44:24, where God declares He was alone "by Myself" when He created

93

the worlds). It is important to note that in these verses (16, 17) the Watchtower Society, in its version, presumptuously adds the word "other" to the text to read "all *other* things" in order to avoid the clear meaning of Paul's words. The *New World Translation of Holy Scriptures* reads, "because by means of him all (other) things were created. . . . All (other) things have been created through him and for him. Also, he is before all (other) things and by means of him all (other) things were made to exist." This demonstrates just how far the Watchtower Society will go in its attempt to deny the deity of the Lord Jesus Christ.

STRAW MAN #3

Proverbs 8:24—Wisdom Brought Forth

Before introducing this Old Testament reference, the Jehovah's Witness will many times begin with the first chapter of I Corinthians, verse 24. There we are told that Christ is the wisdom of God. The Old Testament passage in Proverbs 8 (specifically vv. 24, 25) is then appealed to as clear evidence that Jesus is not eternal since He (wisdom) "was brought forth." However, a closer examination of Proverbs 8 shows that it is not a reference to the Messiah that is intended, since wisdom is referred to in the feminine gender (see vv. 1-3). Proverbs 8 is merely a personification of the trait of wisdom. Furthermore, the erroneousness of the Watchtower's interpretation becomes self-evident if we look closely at Paul's word in I Corinthians 1:24, where Christ is called the "power and wisdom of God." If we hold the Watchtower's viewpoint, then it is clear that there was a time in eternity that Jehovah had *no* power or wisdom. God, however, has always had all the power and wisdom (these are things that make Him God), thus we again see the defectiveness and error of the Society's theology.

STRAW MAN #4

John 1:18—"No Man Hath Seen God at Any Time."

The Jehovah's Witnesses here claim conclusive evidence that Jesus is not and cannot be God, for "no man hath seen God at any time," and people certainly saw Jesus. However, the Witnesses ignore many Old Testament passages where God appeared in some visible form. Notice Genesis 32:30, where Jacob personally encountered God "face to face," and Genesis 18, where the Lord is reported to have visited Abraham. Further occurrences reported are in Genesis 16:13, Exodus 3:6 and Acts 7:2. These incidents recorded in Scripture make clear that the Watchtower application of John's verse is invalid. In fact, John continues by stating that "the only begotten son . . . He has revealed Him." Whenever God appeared to anyone, it was always God's Son who was visibly revealed. Thus the person of God's Son provides the answer to the appearances of God recorded in the Old Testament. This is why Jesus could announce "He who has seen Me has seen the Father" (John 14:9). Christ is God veiled in flesh (Phil. 2:6, 7). Consequently, while no man has seen God the Father (John 6:46) at any time, there have been those who have seen God in the person of His Son, who is the very image of God's substance (Heb. 1:3) and who took upon Him flesh and blood and demonstrated for us God's love and grace.

STRAW MAN #5

John 14:28—"The Father Is Greater Than I"

Here again, the Jehovah's Witnesses use the writings of John and ask, "How could Jesus be God or equal with God when He states that the Father is greater than He?" It should be noted that Jesus stated the Father was *greater* than He, *not better* than He. At this point in Jesus' existence the Father was in a greater position than the Son, since Jesus had humbled Himself and taken the form of a servant (man). He limited Himself, not clinging to His equality with God, and made Himself of no reputation (Phil. 2:6, 7). The term used by Jesus, "greater," denotes position. If Jesus had wished to express inferiority to the Father, He would have stated that the Father is *better* than He. *Better* would have referred to the quality of His nature, not to position. This is what the Watchtower Society would like Jesus to have said. Walter R. Martin, a professor of comparative religions in California, illustrates this important difference: Ronald Reagan is President of the United States and, by virtue of the office he holds, if he were in a group of people he would be "greater" than anyone there. However, Mr. Reagan would be the last to claim that he was "better" than anyone there. *Greater* refers to position, *better* to nature. Jesus Christ was so much better than the angels (Heb. 1:4), since he had *inherited* a more excellent name, that is, *by nature* He was superior to angels. The Watchtower, on the contrary, wishes to reduce God's Son to the stature of a mere angel—Michael the archangel.

STRAW MAN #6

I Corinthians 15:28—"Then Shall the Son Also Himself Be Subject."

The Watchtower here stresses that Christ is inferior by virtue of His being subject to the Father. Subjection is not a synonym for inferiority. Subjection is a form of love. We are told in Ephesians that wives are to submit or be subject unto their husbands. Wives do this because of love for God and their husbands, not because they are inferior to them. Further, the Watchtower interpretation of this verse becomes even more unstable as we examine Luke 2:51, where Jesus was *subject* to Mary and Joseph. Using the Jehovah's Witnesses logic then, we should conclude that Jesus is also inferior to his parents Mary and Joseph. This is contradictory to John 1:3 and Colossians 1:16, 17, where we are told Christ is their Creator. Similarly, the Jehovah's Witnesses use I Corinthians 11:3, where it is stated that the head of Christ is God. Jehovah's Witnesses should note John 16:23, for there *the Father* in essence submits to the Son by fulfilling His wishes and desires, yet this does not imply that the Father is inferior to the Son.

We have dealt with a few of the Jehovah's Witnesses proof texts and hope these will help people to be alert to their misrepresentations of Bible verses. This is a crucial matter, to deny the deity of Christ, which will result in eternal separation from God (John 8:24). Christ is the eternal God revealed in the flesh. All men are commanded to honor the Son just as they honor the Father (John 5:23). Those who do not confess the Son do not have the Father and do not have life (I John 2:23; 5:12).

For further information on misapplied texts of the Watchtower Society, see:

Masters of Deception, F. W. Thomas.
Apostles of Denial, Edmond C. Gruss.
Who's That Knocking at My Door?, Rev. Alex Nova.
Jesus of Nazareth—Who Is He?, Arthur Wallis.

Help in Confronting
The Newer Cults

JOHN P. JUEDES

Editor's Note: John Juedes, a Lutheran pastor in California, is no stranger to *Journal* readers, having shared his research on The Way and on The Holy Order of Mans. He now renders pastors a useful service by presenting us with an annotated bibliography on some of the newer para-Christian groups.

The Divine Light Mission, Edgar Cayce and Jeane Dixon, The Family of Love, International Society for Krishna Consciousness (ISKCON), Transcendental Meditation, The Unification Church, and The Way International have received consideration in some of the more recently published works. The busy pastor, needing quick information on where to find the type of help he needs on one of these sects, will find Pastor Juedes' bibliography a useful guide.

INTRODUCTION

The burgeoning of cults and pseudo-Christian religions in America in the past two decades has forced Christians to respond to their claims. Unfortunately, many Christians either lack information on these groups, or have difficulties determining which resources are most reliable and most helpful for their specific purposes.

This annotated bibliography introduces Christian pastors, leaders, parents, adults and youth to English language material available on the cults. The notations on each of the resources endeavor to supply information and recommendations so that the reader can determine the best resources for his purposes.

An exceptional amount of time and space is necessary to chronicle all of the evangelical Christian, secular and primary printed works on the pseudo-Christian religions. This bibliography focuses on resources offered by evangelical Christian authors and publishers. In addition, some representative and readily available works produced by the cults are summarized. For the purposes of this paper, a cult is defined as a sociologically aberrant religious group or movement. A pseudo-Christian group is defined as a group which appears or is claimed to be Christian or compatible with Christianity, but which close examination reveals is non-Christian in doctrine and practice. For the most part, the groups listed here qualify as both cults and pseudo-Christian religions and are not to be confused with Christian sects or denominations. This bibliography specifically assesses material which addresses these newer, though nationally recognized pseudo-Christian followings: The Divine Light Mission, The Children of God, Edgar Cayce and Jeane Dixon, Hare Krishna, Transcendental Meditation (T.M.), The Unification Church, and The Way International. Some Christian resources address a number of these groups. Chapters of these books are critiqued under their respective group headings. Other resources address the cults as a general topic, mentioning facets of many groups. This bibliography assesses none of these works.

Each pseudo-Christian cult is listed individually, followed by its annotation. The annotation may refer to the cult by the last name of the founder or by an abbreviation of one of its names. The content of each resource is evaluated in the following areas: author's background (including only Ph.D. and accredited theological degrees), history of the group or individual, doctrine, publications, recruitment, sociology, internal difficulties, Christian witness techniques, mood, method, illustrations, documentation and bibliography. When the notations do not mention one of these areas, it is usually because the resource largely neglects it. A use for the resource is often suggested when it is appropriate. To aid the reader, the notations are in list, not paragraph form, and outstanding features are italicized. The notations in this bibliography are consecutively numbered from the first section to the last.

I. THE DIVINE LIGHT MISSION
(Guru Maharaj Ji; a variation—"Spiritual Life Society")

1. Boa, Kenneth. "The Divine Light Mission," *Cults, World Religions, and You*. Wheaton, Ill.: Victor, 1977. Pp. 188-95.
   —*Director of research* for New Life, Inc., graduate, Dallas Theological Seminary.

— *Brief background* on the Guru and DLM organization.
— Notes on recruitment, *indoctrination* and devotee life.
— Evangelically contrasts key Christian doctrines, adds *tips for witnessing*.
— *No documentation* or visuals, 24 entry bibliography on various religions and cults.
— *Leader's guide* available for fruitful group study.

2. Clements, R. D. "The Divine Light Mission," *God and the Gurus.* Downer's Grove, Ill.: InterVarsity, 1975. Pp. 17-24.
— *Ph.D.* from Imperial College, London.
— Sketch of history of the Guru, organization, *distinctive features.*
— Centers on *the "Knowledge"* and language, with some revealing quotations.
— Although DLM section is brief, 42 pages *describe* the basis of DLM, *Hindu Thought,* answering it evangelically and providing direction on how to witness to mystics.
— Exceptional *for any Christian encountering* forms of *Hinduism.*

3. Enroth, Ronald. "The Divine Light Mission," *Youth, Brainwashing and the Extremist Cults.* Grand Rapids, Mich.: Zondervan, 1977. Pp. 133-46.
— *Professor of Sociology* at Westmont College, Ph.D.
— Objectively presented *testimony* of former DLM devotee Jim Ardmore.
— Brief *description* of history, the organization and internal publications.
— Describes recruitment, indoctrination and *mind control* through meditation, rendering one incapable of questioning, reading, or even adding numbers.
— *Ethics* of the group's propensity to lie, and the guru's lifestyle discussed.
— No pictures, *little documentation,* brief bibliography of general cult interest.

4. Larson, Bob. *The Guru.* Denver: Bob Larson Ministries, Box 26438, 1974. 104 pp.
— *Evangelist,* author of books on rock music and the church.
— Experiences at large 1973 *DLM gathering* form the basis.
— History, publication, etc., covered only sporadically.
— Comments on the *psyche of devotees.*

— Contrasts basic practice and *philosophy* from Christianity, with examples of manipulations of Bible passages.
— *Conversational* tone, leaning toward emotional, at times condescending.
— *Digressions* to rock music promotions of forms of Hinduism and to former charlatan Marjoe.
— *32 photographs* of DLM activities and headquarters, moderate documentation, no bibliography.

5. Petersen, William J. "Guru Maharaj Ji and the Divine Light Mission," *Those Curious New Cults*. New Canaan, Conn.: Keats, 1975. Pp. 233-46.
— *Editor of Eternity* magazine.
— Half of this helpful introduction is devoted to the history of the guru and the DLM *organization,* with some critical comments.
— Describes forms of receiving "Knowledge" and *contrasts Christianity* from DLM's form of Hindu teaching and practice.
— Written in *offhand style, little documentation,* no pictures, with concluding bibliography of general cult interest.

6. Sparks, Jack. "Divine Light Mission," *The Mind Benders*. New York: Thomas Nelson, 1977. Pp. 63-89.
— *Christian minister,* former professor of behavioral psychology.
— Introduction to the *history* and method of *operation.*
— Closer look at *recruitment* with the suggestion that its basis is hypnotism.
— Description of *twisting of Scripture* to malign the uniqueness of Jesus and other fundamental Christian doctrines.
— Shows *inconsistency of tenets,* contrasts One Lord Christ with DLM's Lord guru, especially through Christian creeds.
— *Conversational* style, mention of DLM publications, moderate footnoting, no illustrations, 40-entry bibliography of general cult interest.

II. EDGAR CAYCE AND JEANE DIXON

7. Bjornstad, James. *Twentieth Century Prophecy*. Minneapolis: Bethany Fellowship, 1969. 140 pp.
— *Director* of Institute of Contemporary Christianity, *instructor* in philosophy and theology at Northeastern Bible College.

— *Two books in one*—one on Dixon, one on Cayce.

— Describes Dixon's *history, methods* of prediction, true and false *prophecies,* view of the antichrist. Asserts *eight biblical reasons* she cannot be a prophetess of God.

— Details Cayce's *history, readings,* medical genius, true and false *prophecies,*teachings on *Atlantis,* basic theology.

— *Contrasts* Cayce's non-Christian *doctrines* on man, God, hell, the Bible, non-Christian religions, salvation and Jesus *with biblical* teachings.

— *Reviews six books* by Cayce followers, *two appendices* detail Dixon's future prophecies and Dixon's and Cayce's Indo-Aryan, non-Christian worldviews. *Voluminously endnoted* (154 citations on Atlantis alone). No bibliography.

— *Revealing* reading for Christians of any age.

8. Lindsay, Gordon. *Jeane Dixon—Prophetess or Psychic Medium.* Dallas: Christ for the Nations, 1973. 30 pp.

— *Evangelist, founder* of Christ for the Nations.

— Describes origin of and gives *examples of Dixon's power;* illustrates her kind *character.*

— Details *Satan's powers* of prophecy as well as *God's prohibitions* against psychic and occult involvement.

— Concludes that, lacking scriptural knowledge, Dixon and her followers are *deceived by demonic spirits* into believing that her mediumistic powers are a gift of God.

— *Unreferenced quotations* from Montgomery's *A Gift of Prophecy,* some other nonbiblical quotes, many *references to Scripture.* No bibliography or illustrations.

9. Noorbergen, Rene. "Will the Real Jeane Dixon Please Stand Up?," *The Soul Hustlers.* Grand Rapids: Zondervan, 1976. Pp. 113-37.

— *Journalist,* college instructor.

— Substantial *history* of Dixon with a view of her popularity, shows her professed history to be *partially spurious.*

— Applies *four biblical tests* to her prophetic ability: 1) accuracy of her predictions, 2) whether prophecies in Lord's name, 3) changes in visions according to personal whims, 4) personal honesty and credibility.

— Concludes Dixon *fails all four* tests, discounting divine origin of her ability.

— *Substantial documentation* through investigative reporting and unique Psychological Stress Evaluator ("PSE"—*lie detector*) *tests*.

— *Enlightening,* benefits young or adult Christian.

10. Swihart, Phillip J. *Reincarnation, Edgar Cayce and the Bible.* Downers Grove, Ill.: InterVarsity, 1975. 58 pp.

— *Chief psychologist* at Midwestern Colorado Mental Health Center; holds a *doctorate*.

— *Personal history* of Cayce.

— Reveals Cayce's *degrading of scriptural* authority in favor of his readings, and later bendings of Bible verses to support his doctrinal deviations.

— Details *Cayce's doctrines* of creation, the Bible, reincarnation, karma, Jesus, grace, man, judgment and salvation, then *contrasts Bible teaching* in each of these areas.

— Attributes powers to *Satanic influence,* and Cayce only superficially Christian.

— *Appreciable documentation,* no illustrations, no bibliography.

III. THE FAMILY OF LOVE

("Moses" David Berg; former name "Children of God")

11. Enroth, Ronald. "The Children of God," *Youth, Brainwashing, and the Extremist Cults.* Grand Rapids: Zondervan, 1977. Pp. 35-55.

— *Professor of Sociology* at Westmont College; *Ph.D.*

— The *experiences* of former member Janice Evans.

— Brief *history, organization,* and levels of involvement.

— Spotlights *attitudes in COG*—war against "systemites," sexual orientation, greed, lists "litnessing" tips for fundraising.

— Discusses *control* over individuals by gentle pressure resulting in "Moses David robots."

— *Little doctrine,* few footnotes, no photos, outdated statistics, brief bibliography of general cult interest.

— Evangelical author, though this chapter *passes as secular*.

12. Hausmann, Carole, and Gretchen Passantino. "The Children of God (The Family of Love)," *The New Cults,* ed. Walter Martin. Santa Ana, Calif.: Vision House, 1980. Pp. 143-201.

— Hausmann veteran *cult researcher;* Passantino *Research Department Director* for Christian Apologetics: Research and Information Service (C.A.R.I.S.), freelance writer and editor.
— Substantial *up-to-date history,* one weakness being membership estimate.
— Outlines hierarchy, public and private *publications,* and current (not early) *recruitment* technique.
— Critique's *Berg's inconsistency,* prophecy and dictatorial authority.
— Describes *COG doctrine* on God, Jesus, the Holy Spirit, salvation and spiritism, contrasting Bible teaching using much Scripture.
— Details *prominent COG teaching* on revolution, sexual license and anti-Semitism.
— *Extensive quotations,* most from 50 MO Letters in *bibliography* with five other sources, no illustrations.
— This anthology *a "must" for Christian leaders.*

13. Hopkins, Joseph M. "The Children of God: "Disciples of Deception," *Christianity Today.* Feb. 18, 1977, pp. 18-23. (Reprint no. 19)
— *Professor* in the Department of Religion and Philosophy at Westminster College, New Wilmington Pennsylvania; interview of *former members* Jack and Connie Wasson and David Jacks.
— Describes Berg personally and early *history,* detailing the *transformation* from an unusual Jesus People sect to a heretical cult.
— Explains the hierarchical *organization* and sociologically *aberrant attitudes* such as the anti-authority thrusts.
— Details sexual, occult and prophetic *practices,* outlines COG *doctrine* on universalism, authority, marriage, Armageddon, the sacraments, charismatic gifts and day of rest.
— *Quotations* from a number of MO Letters, emphasis on *personal experiences,* some photos, no bibliography.

14. Moriconi, John. *Children of God, Family of Love.* Downers Grove, Ill.: InterVarsity, 1980. 37-pp. booklet.
— *History includes recent developments,* such as the 1978 overhaul of the movement.
— Outlines *contemporary* sexually oriented *recruitment* techniques.
— Emphasizes doctrine, *detailing COG teachings* on Berg's authority, the Godhead, Jesus, the Holy Spirit, occult involvement, reincarnation, antinomianism and spiritual gifts.
— *Rebuts COG teaching* with Scripture.
— *Extensively documented,* almost entirely from MO Letters, the

authoritative writings of the movement.

15. Petersen, William J. "The Children of God and the Jesus Movement," *Those Curious New Cults*. New Canaan, Conn.: Keats, 1975. Pp. 144-60.
   — *Editor of Eternity* magazine.
   — Many details of *early history* as part of the Jesus movement, including names of converts, recruitment and travel.
   — Insights into *early sociological aspects*—hatred for other groups, hard sell, censorship and paranoia. Answers many of these from Scripture.
   — Early writing *misses important later developments*—membership rise and fall, sexual deviations, absolute authority of Berg's MO Letters.
   — Offhand style, *little documentation,* no pictures, concluding 25-entry bibliography of general cults interest.
   — Helpful as *historical study,* but almost worthless as contemporary appraisal of the group.

16. Sparks, Jack. "The Children of God." *The Mind Benders*. New York: Thomas Nelson, 1977. Pp. 155-83.
   — *Christian minister,* former professor of behavioral psychology.
   — Brief *history,* description of fund-raising and *recruitment* in the early days; charges *brainwashing* and difficulty of readjustment confronting former members.
   — Details *COG doctrines* of salvation, end times and worship, refutes COG doctrine of the church.
   — Outdated, *misses newer developments*—restructuring, Flirty-Fishing, the occult and further doctrinal aberrations.
   — *Moderate documentation,* no pictures, concludes with brief outline profile and bibliography of 40 entries of general cult interest.

17. Streiker, Lowell D. "The Children of God," *The Cults Are Coming!* Nashville: Abingdon, 1978. Pp. 50-66.
   — *Director* of the *Mental Health Association* of San Mateo County, California; *Ph.D.*
   — Introduction to *history,* early and later *recruitment* techniques, and the possibility of brainwashing.
   — Outlines some COG attitudes toward *sexual freedom* and *the the occult and occult;* no theology.
   — Discusses *control of followers* by threatening doubters with di-

vine displeasure or ostracism and by the use of out-of-context Bible verses.

— Conversational, some personal knowledge, *moderate documentation* from only four sources (over half from Hopkins above), no bibliography, one drawing.

IV.   INTERNATIONAL SOCIETY FOR KRISHNA CONSCIOUSNESS (ISKCON)
(Swami Prabhupada; also called ''Hare Krishna,'' or ''Krishnas'')

18. Boa, Kenneth. ''The Hare Krishna Movement,'' *Cults, World Religions and You.* Wheaton, Ill.: Victor, 1977. Pp. 178-87.
    — *Director of research* for New Life, Inc.; graduate of Dallas Theological Seminary.
    — Outlines *Indian heritage, history* of the movement, organization and attractions.
    — Describes *temple life.*
    — Outlines *doctrines, contrasting* HK works, karma, reincarnation and character of Krishna with *Christian* salvation and Christ.
    — *Negligible documentation,* no visuals, 24-entry bibliography on various cults and world religions.
    — *Leader's guide* available for fruitful group study.
19. Clements, R. D. ''The Hare Krishna Movement (ISKCON),'' *God and the Gurus.* Downers Grove, Ill.: InterVarsity, 1975. Pp. 25-29.
    — *Ph.D.* from Imperial College, London.
    — Sketch of *history,* the distinctive mantra, ascetic *practices,* scripture, and claim to be the basis of all religions.
    — Concise *quotations* on the purpose and result of chanting.
    — Although the HK section is brief, 42 pages *describe* its basis, *Hindu thought,* answering it evangelically and providing direction on how to witness to mystics.
    — Exceptional *for any Christian encountering* forms of *Hinduism.*
20. Enroth, Ronald. ''The Hare Krishna Movement,'' *Youth, Brainwashing and the Extremist Cults.* Grand Rapids: Zondervan, 1977. Pp. 19-34.
    — *Professor of Sociology* at Westmont College
    — *Objectively presents the experiences* of former devotee Lisa Bryant.

— Insights into attractions of the group and the *psyches of devotees*.

— Focuses on temple *activities*, required conduct and fund raising.

— Details *deception* used by HK to keep Lisa from her evil parents, the *"karmis."*

— Brief history and organization, no doctrine, *little documentation*, no photos, brief bibliography of general cult interest.

— Evangelical author, though this chapter *passes as secular*.

21. Means, Pat. "Hare Krishna: A God in Saffron?," *The Mystical Maze*. N.p.: Campus Crusade for Christ, 1976. Pp. 147-58, 254-57.

— *Campus Crusade for Christ staff* member, lecturer.

— Majority is *systematic* presentation and evangelical refutation of HK *doctrine*.

— Overviews history, *ascetic lifestyle*.

— Spotlights surrender to *hierarchy, deception* in fund raising, view of women, profile of countercultural devotee.

— Offers *tips on witnessing*.

—*Moderate documentation*, seven-entry *bibliography*, one photo.

— While the HK section is brief, the entire 263-page work is an *excellent resource* to aid understanding of and *witness to* Eastern *mystics*, complete with many diagrams and photographs.

22. Miller, Elliot. "Hinduism: Hare Krishna and Transcendental Meditation (TM)," *The New Cults,* ed. Walter Martin. Santa Ana, Calif.: Vision House, 1980. Pp. 79-103.

— Ten-year *veteran of* cult and *apologetic research*, three of these at Martin's Christian Research Institute.

— Historic evolution and multiplicity of Hinduism, spotlighting the *Vedantist school* and the *Bhagavad Gita,* introducing and describing key Sanskrit *Hindu terms*.

— Overviews HK history and *practices*.

— Concisely presents and evanglically *refutes HK doctrines* of God, Christ, salvation and authority.

— Many and *well-chosen quotations,* varied 18-entry *bibliography,* no illustrations.

— This anthology is *a "must" for Christian leaders*.

23. Newport, John P. "The Hare Krishna Movement," *Christ and the New Consciousness*. Nashville, Tenn.: Broadman, 1978. Pp. 30-40.

— Chavanne *Professor* of Religious Studies, Rice University, *Doctorate*.

— Briefly describes *HK doctrines* of the godhead, spiritual master, nature of man, Krishna consciousness and the rituals utilized to attain this. Note that these categories are suggested by the Krishna system rather than imposed on the system by Christian religious patterns.

— History outlines ties to Hinduism and organizational authority; also *details* some dates and events in leader *Probhupada's life* which other works neglect.

— Describes seldom-mentioned *stages of initiation,* as well as the lifestyle and daily schedule of devotees.

— Mentions *secular criticisms* such as mind control, sex segregation, and lack of care for the poor.

— *Moderate documentation* to mainly secular sources, no pictures or bibliography.

— Concise, clear introduction, and details make it useful for some advanced readers. Objectively *secular content* until the Christian response is outlined on the last page.

24. Passantino, Robert and Gretchen, and Raymond Schafer. "Answers to the Hare Krishnas," *Answers to the Cultists at Your Door*. Eugene, Ore.: Harvest House, 1981. Pp. 139-57.

— Passantinos are *veterans of cult ministry* and writing, former research associates at Christian Research Institute, now are directors of Christian Apologetics: Research and Information Service; Schafer writes and edits.

— Sketch treatment of Indian and American history, outlines the cult lifestyle of a former member, indicates rationale behind fund raising and its accompanying *"transcendental trickery"* (deception).

— Very brief statements of *HK doctrine* in the areas of God, Jesus Christ, the Holy Spirit, mankind, and salvation, with biblical refutation of each.

— Engaging style, especially suits the *light reader,* skeletal treatment.

— *Little documentation,* no pictures, 49-entry bibliography of general cult interest, index of Scripture passages quoted in all chapters.

25. Petersen, William J. "Hare Krishna," *Those Curious New Cults*. New Canaan, Conn.: Keats, 1975. Pp. 163-73.

— *Editor of Eternity* magazine.

— Describes *early history* and converts in America.

— Spotlights *HK emphases,* differentiates from some similarly

107

sounding "Krishna" movements.
— Supports four *sociological reasons youth join.*
— Offhand style of writing, *little documentation,* no pictures, with concluding 25-entry bibliography of general cult interest.

26. Prabhupada, A. C. Bhaktivedanta, Swami. *On the Way to Krishna.* New York: Bhaktivedanta Book Trust, 1973. 79pp.
— *Founder of ISKCON.*
— *Emphasizes* that happiness is not the material world, and that to be happy all must serve and accurately worship *Krishna,* who is lauded throughout Prabhupada's writings.
— Direct, *clear style, many illustrations* from nature; many excerpts from the *Bhagavad Gita* in Sanskrit transliteration and English.
— No documentation (outside the *Gita*) or bibliography, one drawing, *two photos.*

27. Sparks, Jack. "Hare Krishna," *The Mind Benders.* New York: Thomas Nelson, 1977. Pp. 91-118.
— *Christian minister,* former professor of behavioral psychology.
— Substantial American *history.*
— *Systematically describes doctrines* of God, creation, man, purpose of life, and salvation, contrasting Christian teaching on authority, God, salvation and reincarnation.
— Details *public activities* and *private temple practices.*
— *Conversational* style appeals especially to youth.
— *Little documentation,* no pictures, 40-entry bibliography of general cult interest, concludes with profile outline of the group.

28. Streiker, Lowell D. "Hare Krishna!," *The Cults Are Coming!* Nashville: Abingdon, 1978. Pp. 67-95.
— *Director* of the *Mental Health Association* of San Mateo County, California; *Ph.D.*
— Outlines Hindu *tradition,* American history, organization and membership statistics; describes *Back to Godhead* magazine; *no doctrine.*
— Focuses on local temple practices and *activities of devotees,* especially marriage practice, commune life and four main rules of conduct.
— Offers *stages of involvement* leading to initiation, includes profiles of and testimonies by devotees.
— Conversational, based on *personal knowledge,* some documentation, no bibliography, four photographs.

V. TRANSCENDENTAL MEDITATION
(Maharishi Mahesh Yogi; commonly called "T.M.")

29. Bjornstad, James. *The Transcendental Mirage*. Minneapolis: Bethany Fellowship, 1976. 93 pp.
    — *Director* of Institute of Contemporary Christianity, *instructor* in philosophy and theology at Northeastern Bible College.
    — Evangelical introduction shows *TM's religious nature*, presents its Indian heritage in passing.
    — Presents TM's *lofty claims*, some contrasting research, and describes *dangers* inherent in meditation.
    — Contrasts its basic religious views from Christian doctrine using five *diagrams*.
    — Varied, 25-entry bibliography, *substantial documentation, helpful appendices* present the puja text in English, Yogi's interpretation of Scripture with refutation and telling changes in TM organization and promotion in the 60's.
    — Direct, data and diagrams very useful for *Christian teachers*.

30. Boa, Kenneth. "Transcendental Meditation," *Cults, World Religions, and You*. Wheaton, Ill.: Victor, 1977. Pp. 156-66.
    — *Director of research* for New Life, Ind.; graduate of Dallas Theological Seminary.
    — Sketches *historical background*, including spiritual aims at its American introduction.
    — Outlines *esoteric Hindu teachings*, unfulfilled claims and problems in meditation.
    — Contrasts *underlying philosophy* on God, ignorance and karma with Christian views.
    — *No documentation* or visuals, 24-entry bibliography on various religions and cults.
    — *Leader's guide* available for fruitful group study.

31. Carlson, Ronald L. *Transcendental Meditation: Relaxation or Religion?* Chicago: Moody, 1978. 156 pp.
    — *Evangelist* and *lecturer* on the cults.
    — *Emphasizes philosophy*—American, Hindu (especially Vedanta and Yoga) and TM's place in Hindu philosophy.
    — Substantial, *revealing history* and statistics, outlines recruitment program.

— Thorough *treatment of the mantra* in Indian and TM use.

— Describes underlying *Hindu philosophy* with many references to *esoteric documents* such as the Holy Tradition and Puja.

— *Documentation extensive,* as is the balanced 83-entry *bibliography;* chart of TM mantras.

— Seventeen-page Addendum outlining *Christian meditation.*

— Emphasis on philosophy best suits *better educated* individuals.

32. Clements, R. D. "Transcendental Meditation," *God and the Gurus.* Downer's Grove, Ill.: InterVarsity, 1975. Pp. 30-34.

— *Ph.D.* from Imperial College, London.

— Skeleton history and *distinctive features.*

— Interesting *quotations* on the "unmanifest" Creative Intelligence.

— The age of the article is shown by lack of scientific data on the physiological impact of TM and old fee scale.

— Although the TM section is brief, 42 pages *describe* the basis of TM, *Hindu thought,* answering it evangelically, and providing direction on how to witness to mystics.

— Exceptional *for any Christian encountering forms of Hinduism,* especially "hardcore" rather than beginning meditators.

33. Gerberding, Kieth A. *How to Respond to Transcendental Meditation.* St. Louis: Concordia Publishing House, 1977. 31 pp.

— Parish *pastor* (former campus pastor), religious writer, *Th.D.*

— Presents *lofty claims* made by TM, offers Christianity as option.

— Asserts that *TM is religious,* though spends little space demonstrating it.

— Spotlights *unmet personal needs* that attract people to TM.

— Good section on *Christian meditation,* although almost seems to leave door open to a version of "Christianized" TM.

— Moderate documentation for its size, seven-entry bibliography, no illustrations, *slightly redundant.*

— *Contrasts TM with Christianity, defines the basics,* challenges Christianity to reach out to meet people's spiritual hunger.

34. Haddon, David, and Vail Hamilton. *TM Wants You!* Grand Rapids: Baker, 1976. 204 pp.

— Haddon *writes articles* on TM for prominent evangelical magazines, Hamilton is a *former TM instructor.*

— A voluminously *detailed history* of TM's Indian origins and development in America.

— *Personal knowledge and experiences* and conversational *question and answer format* makes interesting and informative reading.

— Reveals conflicting *scientific data* on the physiological usefulness of TM.

— Devastating critiques of the real *nature of "enlightenment"* brought about by meditation, its source in faith, not seeing and the necessity of meditation to *alter perception* in order to accept Hindu monistic worldview.

— *Extensive personal experience,* secular and scriptural *documentation,* though no bibliography or illustrations.

— Very *thorough,* interests any reader.

35. Lewis, Gordon R. *What Everyone Should Know About Transcendental Meditation.* Glendale, Calif.: G/L, 1975. 95 pp.

— *Professor* at Conservative Baptist Theological Seminary, Denver, *Ph.D.*

— *Brief history* of Yogi and the organization, describes initiation ceremony.

— Presents *claims, refutes* some from secular sources, offers two testimonies of former meditators.

— Thorough *description of TM, (Hindu) theology,* contrasting Christian theology using word illustrations and much Scripture.

— Thirteen-page *glossary* of terms, substantial *documentation,* varied, 37-entry *bibliography,* no visuals.

— *Proposes Christian meditation,* resistance to public funding for TM.

— Especially helpful for *uninformed Christians* of any age.

36. Miller, Elliot. "Hinduism: Hare Krishna and Transcendental Meditation (TM)," *The New Cults,* ed. Walter Martin. Santa Ana, Calif.: Vision House, 1980. Pp. 79-103.

— Ten-year *veteran of cult* and apologetic *research,* three of these at Christian Research Institute.

— Historic evolution and multiplicity of Hinduism, spotlighting the *Vedantist school* and the Bhagavad Gita, introducing some key Sanskrit *Hindu terms.*

— Outlines *history,* organization and *scientific research* which reveals meditation's shortfalls.

— Demonstrates its *religious nature,* examines religious ceremony and mantras and the New Jersey *court decision* which declared its religious nature.

111

— Contrasts *TM doctrines* of God, Christ and salvation with Christian doctrines.

— Many and *well-chosen quotations,* varied 18-entry *bibliography,* no illustrations.

— This anthology is a "must" *for Christian leaders.*

37. Patton, John E. *The Case Against TM in the Schools.* Grand Rapids: Baker, 1976. 100 pp.

— Original *plaintiff counsel* in 1977 case Malnak vs. Yogi.

— Written as a *brief* for the above case.

— Substantial *introduction to Hinduism* and appreciable data on *Yogi in India.*

— Invaluable section on TM's original *spiritual goals* and the *conspiracy* by TM leaders to obscure its religious nature.

— Demonstrates *religious nature* of TM writings and practices *quoting rare publications* such as The Holy Tradition, English puja, teacher contract, early writings of Yogi and high school texts.

— Applies *First Amendment law* to its promotion in public school.

— *Extensive documentation* on sometimes lengthy quotations, no bibliography or illustrations.

— *Revealing, occasional sophisticated* language, assumes a general knowledge of TM, good for secular use and further study.

38. Petersen, William J. "Transcendental Meditation and the Maharishi Mahesh Yogi," *Those Curious New Cults.* New Canaan, Conn.: Keats, 1975. Pp. 185-95.

— *Editor of Eternity* magazine.

— Describes the *early movements* and followers of the Yogi.

— Deals with TM as a simplistic, *deficient way to attain bliss* and offers the better Christian alternative.

— Does not address the all-important area of *TM's philosophical underpinnings* and religious nature.

— Written in *offhand style, little documentation,* no pictures, with concluding 25-entry bibliography of general cult interest.

39. Scott, R. D. *Transcendental Misconceptions.* San Diego: Beta, 1978. 227 pp.

— Six years in TM as meditator and instructor.

— Revolves around author's *personal experiences* of getting into TM, observing its systematic deception, and his resulting departure.

— Exposé of TM's *"dishonesty and deception* originating with Maharishi Mahesh Yogi himself'' permeating its theory, practice, and promotion.

— Many insights into the *early days* of the movement in America, and into the *psyche of the instructor*.

— Reveals TM deception *regarding the mantras*—their selection, evolution, code names for deities, expansions into worship phrases.

— Thorough treatment (30 pp.) of *demonic possession* brought about by practice of TM with specific reference to Scripture.

— *Evangelical orientation* offers some comparison of Christ's teachings with Maharishi's teachings.

— *Weak objective documentation,* no bibliography or illustrations.

— *Six invaluable appendices* include the text of the secret and generally unavailable ''Holy Tradition,'' testimonies of former TM instructors and the scientific case against TM.

— Scott's exposé *enthralls any reader, appendices* excellent for *advanced study*.

40. *TM in Court.* Berkeley, Calif.: Spiritual Counterfeits Project, 1978. 75 pp.

— *The Honorable H. Curtis Meanor* of the U.S. District Court, Newark.

— The *Court's opinion* in the case of Malnak vs. Yogi (1977), concludes that although the ''defendants' teachings wear novel labels,'' they are undoubtedly religious.

— *Meticulously examines* the TM high school *textbook* as well as the initiatory *puja* ceremony.

— Analyzes and *rejects TM arguments* that they are not religious, noting inconsistencies between the facts and TM testimony.

— *Voluminous documentation* of the text as well as affadavits and puja.

— Applies American law, highly *technical* language hinders the average reader, no bibliography or illustrations.

— *Invaluable* as landmark secular appraisal of TM as religious; especially useful to demonstrate the religious nature of TM to *non-Christians*.

41. Weldon, John, and Zola Levitt. *The Transcendental Explosion.* Irvine, Calif.: Harvest House, 1976. 218 pp.

— One time research editor, now on *faculty* of The Light and Power House, ''Biblical Training School,'' Westwood, California. Levitt—*author,* talk show host.

— Sketches scientific *promotional front* and enticement of individual and world utopia, *branches* and effectiveness of the organization.
— Extensive discussions of *negative* and antisocial *effects of meditation*—personality alteration leading sometimes to insanity and suicide.
— Details TM's religious nature, contrasting its Hindu traditions with Christian teaching on meditation, God, sin, Jesus and His work, death and life.
— *Devastating appendices* tie mantras to Hindu deities, TM to occult and yoga dangers and rebuts reincarnation.
— Demonstrates that *science* has not proven TM's claimed benefits. Revealing, *extensive footnoting,* no bibliography or illustrations.
— Thorough treatment of innate dangers of TM, for *advanced readers*.

Ed. note: A handy summary of TM for busy pastors can be found in "TM: A Pagan Way of Thinking," *Journal of Pastoral Practice* I, 1 (1977): 138-46.

VI. THE UNIFICATION CHURCH
(Sun Myung Moon; also called "Moonies," or the "Holy Spirit Association for the Unification of World Christianity")

42. Bjornstad, James. *The Moon is Not the Son*. Minneapolis: Bethany Fellowship, 1976. 125 pp.
— *Director* of Institute of Contemporary Christianity, *instructor* in philosophy and theology at Northeastern Bible College; *Ph.D*.
— General *history* with *some seldom mentioned facts,* especially regarding ritual sex.
— Mentions and quotes both general and *in-house* Moon *publications*.
— Describes and extensively refutes both *general and esoteric doctrine*.
— *Six charts* contrast Moon doctrine with Christianity in key areas of God, the world, sin, salvation and the Messiah.
— Discusses recruitment and the *sociology* of brainwashing as well as problems in revelations.
— Encourages and supplies method for *witnessing* by author's example.

— Testimony of former Moonie in appendix, extensive and revealing *endnotes* with 24-entry bibliography.

— Invaluable for *Christian teachers* and leaders as introduction or for reference.

43. Boa, Kenneth. "The Unification Church," *Cults, World Religions, and You*. Wheaton, Ill.: Victor, 1977. Pp. 167-77.

— *Director of research* for New Life, Inc.; graduate, Dallas Seminary.

— Brief *critical history;* describes "love-bombing" recruitment, details basic *doctrine* in contrast to Christianity, with a warning to the Christian church.

— Lists reasons for *government investigations*, details *"progressive esoterism,"* the basis of the indoctrination/brainwashing program.

— *No documentation* or visuals, 24-entry bibliography on various religions and cults.

— *Leader's guide* available for fruitful group study.

44. Enroth, Ronald. "The Unification Church," *Youth, Brainwashing and the Extremist Cults*. Grand Rapids: Zondervan, 1977. Pp. 97-121.

— *Professor of sociology* at Westmont College; Ph.D.

— Objectively presents the moving *experiences* of former Moonie Shelly Liebert without emphasizing the sensational.

— Excellent insight into *life in the Unification Church,* the psyche of a Moonie, "choreographed" recruitment, lifestyle of Rev. Moon, and esoteric teachings.

— Includes excerpts from some *in-house Moon documents*.

— *Little doctrine* or history, no footnotes or photos, brief bibliography of general cult interest.

— Evangelical author, though this chapter could *pass as secular*.

45. Levitt, Zola. *The Spirit of Sun Myung Moon*. Irvine, Calif.: Harvest House, 1976. 127 pp.

— *Author,* lecturer, radio talk show host.

— Emphasizes the emotional and *spectacular to distraction*.

— *Minor* treatment of *history* and doctrine.

— Offhand, *almost pejorative* style depending largely on his and others' testimonies.

— The evangelical presentation is strong on *America's place in Moon theology* and Moon recruitment techniques.

— Lacks bibliography and illustrations; *little documentation*.

46. Moon, Sun Myung. *Divine Principle,* trans. Wolli Haeje. 2nd ed.

Washington: Holy Spirit Association for the Unification of World Christianity, 1973. 536 pp.

— *Founder of the Moonies,* considered Messiah by some.

— *Considered* (part of) the *"new truth"*; and essentially scripture by Moonies, teaching that the Bible is but a "textbook" containing much symbolism and "secret meaning."

— Detailed 12-page table of contents, three *historical time-event charts* covering Judeo-Christian history to its culmination in the present "Lord of the Second Advent."

— Systematically covers *all major doctrines,* including the principle of creation, fall of man, attempted consummations of human history, advent, failure and resurrection of the Messiah, Christology, predestination, foundation of restoration, ages in history, description of and preparation for the second advent of the Messiah.

— *Deletes* or only infers *esoteric* doctrines, such as Moon as the Messiah.

— Many references to *Bible verses,* most interpreted far differently than common Christian views.

— *Lacks non-biblical documentation,* no bibliography, photo of Moon as frontispiece.

— *Clearly written,* though philosophy is at times complicated; helpful for *advanced* reading or reference for researchers.

47. Newport, John P. "The Unification Church," *Christ and the New Consciousness.* Nashville, Tenn.: Broadman, 1978. Pp. 119-39.

— Chavanne *Professor* of Religious Studies, Rice University, *Doctorate.*

— *Substantial history* includes many names, dates, notes on organization. Helpful *statistics* on property and membership in three nations.

— Details *teachings* on Taoistic duality, especially in relation to God, the fall as a result of sexual acts, communism, Jesus' failure as Messiah, Moon as the new messiah, and marriage and perfection. Mentions Oriental, occult, and patriotic *influences.*

— Helpful discussion of the nature and practice of *mind control* and *deprogramming* and their relation to *religious freedom.*

— *Lifestyle* and *recruitment* of Moonies described primarily by testimony of former member.

— *Secular criticisms* such as deceptive Unification Church practices,

—mind control, financial holdings and five sources of them, ties to Korean government.

— Christian *theological evaluation* in six main areas, includes notes on Moon distortions of the Bible.

— *Extensive footnotes* from a range of sources, though no bibliography or pictures. Concise, thorough introduction would benefit some more advanced readers.

48. Passantino, Robert and Gretchen, Raymond Schafer. "Answers to the Moonies," *Answers to the Cultist at Your Door.* Eugene, Ore.: Harvest House, 1981. Pp. 121-38.

— Passantinos are *veterans of cult ministry* and writing, former research associates at Christian Research Institute, now are directors of Christian Apologetics: Research and Information Service; Schafer writes and edits.

— Brief treatment of history, *touches on* only two of the many *secular criticisms* of the Unification Church.

— Weak, *unbalanced picture of Moon theology,* few, sometimes feeble quotations are forced into categories suggested by Christian thought. Moon doctrines on the Bible, God, Jesus Christ, the Holy Spirit, and salvation are *biblically answered.*

— Hints on how to respond to Moonies given, especially in *testimony* of a former Moonie.

— *Little documentation,* no pictures, 49-entry bibliography of general cult interest, index of Scripture passages quoted in all chapters. Aimed at the light reader.

49. Petersen, William J. "Sun Myung Moon," *Those Curious New Cults.* New Canaan, Conn.: Keats, 1975. Pp. 247-61.

— *Editor* of *Eternity* magazine.

— Junior high on up would benefit from this brief but superb introduction to the Unification Church's *history and doctrine.*

— Insight into *roots* in *Eastern* religions and *spiritistic* phenomena.

— In objective evangelical manner Petersen points out major *deviations from Christian theology.*

— Brief general bibliography but unfortunately *lacks documentation* and pictures.

— Helpful at *any age.*

50. Sontag, Frederick. *Sun Myung Moon and the Unification Church.* Nashville: Abingdon, 1977. 224 pp.

— *Professor of philosophy* at Pomona College, *Ph.D.*

— Revolves around Sontag's pleasant *experiences at Moon communes* around the world, providing insights into the global movement.
— Thirty pages of flattering *testimonies of Moonies.*
— Toleration and *support for Moon,* multiple pages attacking deprogramming, few "concessions" to opponents' charges.
— Theologically liberal *reflections,* concluding that aberrant doctrine and negative experiences of some do not discount benefits to others.
— Largely undocumented except for *overview of* the *Divine Principle* and eight pages of Master Speaks excerpts.
— Thirty-page *interview with Moon* plus "Theological Affirmations."
— *Comprehensive bibliography* of 54 books and over 125 articles in seven categories; 66 photographs.

51. Sparks, Jack. "The Unification Church of Sun Myung Moon," *The Mind Benders.* New York: Thomas Nelson, 1977. Pp.121-53.
— *Christian minister,* former professor of behavioral psychology.
— Emphasizes *Moon doctrine* in critical areas, and biblically refutes each.
— Includes mention of some *esoteric practices,* history, recruitment, sociology, and *Eastern roots* of the doctrine.
— *Conversational* style, lacks documentation, 40-entry bibliography of general cult interest, no pictures.
— Good doctrinal introduction concludes with *profile* outline.

52. Streiker, Lowell D. "The Unification Church of Sun Myung Moon," *The Cults Are Coming!* Nashville: Abingdon, 1978. Pp. 20-49.
— *Director of the Mental Health Association* of San Mateo County, California. *Ph.D.*
— Brief overview of *doctrine,* but no mention of history.
— Concern "is more with *how* the Moonies teach than with *what* they teach"; describing the attraction, progressive indoctrination, use of *mind control and coercive pressure* used to make and hold converts.
— Negligible documentation, revolves around *former Moonie* Mike and *opinion of* Samuel Klein, *Ph.D.*
— A *weak* introduction with *no distinctive offerings.*

53. Yamamoto, J. Isamu. *The Puppet Master.* Downer's Grove, Ill.: Inter-Varsity, 1977. 136 pp.

— *Researcher and lecturer* for Spiritual Counterfeits Project, Berkeley, California.
— Most *comprehensive* of evangelical offerings; *extensive* detailed *history* of Moon and the Church with many critical comments.
— Well organized, with special chapters on *recruitment* and *operation* of the Unified Family, on *political* operations.
— *Doctrine* includes the seldom-mentioned tenets such as marriage, and *esoteric* teachings.
— Description of and many quotations from *in-house publications* such as *Master Speaks*.
— Exhortation to *witness* with discussion of method and deprogramming as well as Moon's place in Satan's overall objectives for the world.
— Four simple *diagrams* of Moon theology plus the church emblem.
— *Extensive documentation*, though no bibliography.
— Much *advanced information*, but usable as a comprehensive introduction.

VII. THE WAY INTERNATIONAL
(Victor Paul Wierwille; also called "Wayers")

54. Boa, Kenneth. "The Way International," *Cults, World Religions, and You*. Wheaton, Ill.: Victor, 1977. Pp. 196-203.
— *Director of research* for New Life, Inc.; graduate, Dallas Theological Seminary.
— Helpful *overview* of history and basic teachings.
— Reveals its *second authority* which "systematically distorts" Scripture to produce "Wierwillism."
— Evangelically contrasts Christian doctrines of God, Christ, the Holy Spirit and salvation, offering *tips for witnessing*.
— *No documentation* or visuals, 24-entry bibliography on various religions and cults.
— *Leader's guide* available for fruitful group study.
55. Enroth, Ronald. "The Way," *Youth, Brainwashing and the Extremist Cults*. Grand Rapids: Zondervan, 1977. Pp. 122-32.
— *Professor of sociology* at Westmont College; Ph.D.
— Objectively presents the *experiences* of former Wayer Marie Leonetti.

— Good insight into The Way's techniques of recruitment and *progressive indoctrination* which create "a little Way robot."

— *Brief history* and organization, mention of some doctrines.

— *Little documentation,* no photos, with a brief bibliography of general cult interest.

— Evangelical author, though this chapter *passes as secular.*

56. Juedes, John. "Trinitarianism—A Pagan Creation? An Examination of Dr. Victor Paul Wierwille's Claim," *The Journal of Pastoral Practice* V, 2 (1981): 67-82.

— Lutheran *Pastor, M.Div.*

— Specializes in *refuting V. P. Wierwille's claim that the Trinity is a pagan creation,* not truly Christian doctrine. Detailed examination of chapter 1 of Wierwille's book, *Jesus Christ is Not God,* which poses an anti-trinitarian view of church history.

— Evangelical, objective, *extgensive footnotes* focus on sources Wierwille cites and on writings of early church fathers, *addendum* refutes Wierwille's view that Martin Luther was anti-trinitarian.

— Easy to follow, *useful also for response to other anti-trinitarian cults* such as Jehovah's Witnesses.

57. Juedes, John. "Wierwille's Way with the Word," *The Journal of Pastoral Practice* IV, 1 (1980):89-120. Offprinted by Personal Freedom Outreach.

— Lutheran *pastor, M.Div.*

— Evangelical, objectively presented, *overlooks* the usual categories of *history,* and systematic presentation and refutation of doctrine.

— *Assesses only* The Way's interpretation of Scripture, revealing extensive inaccuracies in use of Greek words, language and text.

— *Extensive footnotes* with two charts and a six-page *addendum* of parallels between V. P. Wierwille's *Receiving the Spirit Today* and E. W. Bullinger's *The Giver and His Gifts.*

— *Assumes substantial knowledge* of exegetical theology or Way doctrine.

— Especially useful *for church leaders* to rescue someone from The Way by demonstrating corruption in the key area of scholarship.

58. Morton Douglas. "Ancient Heresies Modernized," *The Journal of Pastoral Practice* IV, 1 (1980): 73-88. Offprinted by Personal Freedom Outreach.

— Lutheran *pastor, M.Div.*

— Good introduction contains *substantial history* with some critical notes.

— Evangelically *refutes* the key Way *doctrines of Jesus Christ and holy spirit.*

— *Extensive footnotes* contain *a gold mine* of information and disprove some important Way assertions.

— Unfortunately does not address more doctrines and lacks pictures but includes *addendum* on Martin Luther and The Way.

— *Footnotes* and some content would best benefit the *more able readers.*

59. Passantino, Robert and Gretchen, Raymond Schafer, ''Answers to the Way International,'' *Answers to the Cultist At Your Door.* Eugene, Ore.: Harvest House, 1981. Pp. 159-82.

— Passantinos are *veterans of cult ministry* and writing, former research associates at Christian Research Institute, now are directors of Christian Apologetics: Research and Information Service; Schafer writes and edits.

— Sketches *history, organization,* emphases, and testimony of a former Way follower.

— Briefly states and biblically *refutes Way stances* on the biblical interpretation and autographs, the Trinity, Jesus Christ, the Holy Spirit, the nature of man, and salvation—especially its relationship to speaking in tongues.

— *Suggestions on how to witness* to Way followers, and on which Bible passages clearly state the orthodox Christian doctrine.

— Clear introduction to The Way, some documentation, no pictures, 49-entry bibliography of general cult interest, *index of some passages quoted* in all chapters.

60. Sparks, Jack. ''The Way International,'' *The Mind Benders.* New York: Thomas Nelson, 1977. Pp. 185-218.

— *Christian minister,* former professor of behavioral psychology.

— *Conversational introduction* includes brief history with some critical notes and all important doctrines.

— Describes techniques and *''gimmicks'' of recruitment* and brainwashing.

— Strong refutation of *Way misuse of early church history,* but could use much more Scripture to refute group's doctrines.

— *Lacks* more *recent data* on organization and facilities.

— *Moderate documentation,* no pictures, concludes with brief outline profile and bibliography of 40 entries of general cult interest.

— Helpful *especially for youth* to understand main differences from historical Christianity.

61. Van Gordon, Kurt. "The Way International," *The New Cults*, ed. Walter Martin. Santa Ana, Calif.: Vision House, 1980. Pp. 37-78.

— *Director* of Practical Apologetics and Christian Evangelism (P.A.C.E.), onetime missionary for Christian Research Institute.

— *Substantial history* with critical notes; reviews basic teachings on God, the Bible, the person and work of Christ, the Holy Spirit, man and salvation

— *Logical refutations* of fallacious arguments and doctrinal inconsistencies; substantial critique of Way use of Aramaic.

— Offers *biblical passages* which contradict Way doctrine.

— *Much documentation*, nine-entry bibliography of primary sources, no illustrations.

— Exceptionally thorough and *revealing introduction* using sometimes sophisticated theological language.

62. Wierwille, Victor Paul. *Power for Abundant Living*. New Knoxville, Ohio: American Christian, 1971. 368 pp.

— *Founder of The Way International, Th.M.*

— Introduces many of The Way's *peculiar and heretical teachings* such as non-deity of Christ, Aramaic New Testament originals, soul sleep, four men crucified with Christ, ultradispensationalism, holy spirit and the fall.

— Claims to teach Bible accuracy and how the Bible interprets itself, yet it is permeated with severe *errors of scholarship*, especially in his use of biblical languages (see "Wierwille's Way With the Word" above for examples).

— Characteristic of Wierwille's preachy *Bible study style* with many biblical excerpts and denunciations of denominational churches.

— Many apparent *borrowings from* E. W. Bullinger's *How to Enjoy the Bible* (1913).

— *Without* any *documentation*, bibliography or illustrations.

63. Williams, J. L. *Victor Paul Wierwille and The Way International*. Chicago: Moody, 1979. 158 pp.

— *Director* of The New Directions Evangelistic Association, *M.Div.*

— *Substantial history* with some critical notes; much on the hierarchical organization.

— Presents characteristic doctrine with extensive *evangelical treat-*

ment of the teachings on Christ, the Trinity and the Holy Spirit.

— Substantial refutation of Way *use of church history,* many notes on inaccurate Way *scholarship* with *extensive documentation* overall.

— Some personal testimonies, sincerity and concern with sketches of encouragement to and *method of Christian witness.*

— Many *revealing quotations* of Wierwille from an Art Toalston interview which are unavailable elsewhere.

— No pictures, but lists cult resource groups, with *19 pages of appendices* of scriptural passages on Christ and the Trinity.

— Postscript of Marks of Cults, 18-entry *bibliography* plus 17-book reading list. Helpful as thorough introduction or advanced.

BOOK REVIEW

Lawrence Foster. *Religion and Sexuality: Three American Communal Experiments of the Nineteenth Century* (New York and Oxford: Oxford University Press, 1981). Pp. xi + 363. Reviewed by John E. Thompson.

Lawrence Foster has given us an important book on a very difficult subject. Based on his 1976 Ph.D. dissertation at the University of Chicago, this thorough and illuminating study of Shaker celibacy, Oneida Community complex marriage, and Mormon polygamy is probably destined long to remain a standard work. With extensive footnotes (alone worth the price of the book) and an essay on sources, *Religion and Sexuality* is a valuable resource for researchers in the field. At the same time, it is an enjoyable book, which anyone could read with profit.

Foster uses a sophisticated comparative approach and profitably engages the insights of disciplines as disparate as psychology, sociology, religion and history. Foster's goal is to understand the social innovations of these groups as not merely religious, but also as a response to the great social changes taking place in America at the beginning of the nineteenth century. They are, as Foster sees it, radical products of the great revivals, as basicially conservative, and yet, paradoxically, radically changing.

Moving on now to a discussion of Mormon polygamy, and, in particular, the matter of its origin, Foster rejects four hypotheses regarding the beginnings of polygamy outright as too sim-plistic. They are: 1) the view of the Reorganized Church of Jesus Christ of Latter Day Saints that Joseph Smith, Jr., never practiced polygamy during his life time; 2) the anti-Mormon view that the introduction of polygamy was nothing but the result of an over-active libido, even while Foster allows that "no serious scholar would deny that sex drives influenced the introduction of polygamy"; 3) the Mormon view that polygamy was solely the result of a commandment from heaven, since it does not consider adequately the means by which the Prophet often sought revelation; and 4) psychological reductionisms. Foster concludes, from his naturalistic perspective as a non-believer in Joseph Smith's work, that any explanation of the origin of polygamy that neglects the Prophet's personal sense of religious mission, regardless of what one thinks about that mission, is inadequate. Christians engaged in a study of the origin of Mormon polygamy could profit from Foster's observation on this point.

There are few surprises in Foster's treatment of polygamy during the lifetime of the Prophet (1831–1844). He argues that Joseph was trying to establish the doctrine, and perhaps, even the practice of polygamy as early as 1831.

At the same time, Foster admits that most practice of the principle was actually restricted to the Nauvoo period (1841–1844). The public denials of polygamy in the face of private practice (beginning as early as 1835 and continuing as late as 1844) were, Foster thinks, politically necessary while purposely evasive, if not dishonest. Foster's work on the John Cook Bennett Affair (1842) is an excellent example of how cautiously to untangle a very complicated story in search of what actually happened. After reading Foster, one almost feels he finally understands both the Prophet and Bennett, perhaps for the first time.

Chapter 5, entitled " 'Puritan Polygamy': Brigham Young and the Institutionalization of Mormon Polygamy, 1844–1852," might, very properly, receive another title, since the period it covers extends all the way to the Manifesto of 1890, which set aside polygamy. Otherwise, it is an excellent piece of work. His survey of the struggle of the various Mormon schismatic groups with the principle of polygamy is brief, but extremely worthwhile. His extended discussion of the story of Mrs. Franklin S. Richards' life as a polygamous wife will go far to break down many preconceptions of what life was like in polygamous Utah.

Foster's discussion of Mormon polygamy, then, is sympathetic in its description of the human factor, and yet, at the same time, compellingly honest and critical. It is appropriate that the first work on Mormon polygamy by a non-Mormon who had been granted full access to the holdings of the LDS Archives on the subject should have been done by a scholar of such depth and ability as Dr. Foster. One hopes that Foster's work will be the first in a long series of such studies on all aspects of Mormon history. It is clear that non-Mormon scholarship can make a real contribution to the study of Mormon history. It is to be hoped that more non-Mormons, especially evangelical Christians, will see fit to do so.

In conclusion, there is only one matter I wish Foster would have discussed, which he chose not to. That is whether the ideas of Joseph Smith on polygamy, in their formative stage, might be traced back even further than the 1831 revelation on marrying Lamanites, even beyond the foundation of the Church of Christ on April 6, 1830, or the publication of *The Book of Mormon* the previous month. Admittedly, the evidence for such an idea is sketchy, like the tip of an iceberg sticking just barely above the water level. Indeed, at the present time, I know of only one piece of evidence for this idea, but it is worth considering. Levi Lewis, of Harmony, Pennsylvania, in an affidavit referred to in Eber D. Howe's *Mormonism Unvailed* (1834 ed., p. 268), states that Joseph Smith Jr. and Martin Harris once told him that "adultery is no crime" and that the Prophet attempted to seduce a girl named Eliza Winters. It may be, that when all is said and done, just such an incident may prove to be the earliest example of both the doctrine and practice of Mormon polygamy by the Prophet. We need to know more.

NEWS NOTES

SUPREME COURT ALLOWS LIMITS TO
FUND—RAISING BY RELIGIOUS GROUPS

States may limit soliciting and literature distribution by religious groups, the Supreme Court has ruled.

Such limits are constitutional when a "significant governmental interest" in the "safety and convenience" of people in a public forum is shown, the court ruled.

The specific case involved members of the International Society of Krishna Consciousness and a challenge to a Minnesota law preventing members of the sect from roaming the Minnesota State Fairgrounds, distributing literature and seeking contributions.

The Krishna group said the law was a violation of their rights to freely exercise their religion, specifically the practice of "sankirtan," a ritual requiring members to distribute literature and seek contributions.

While the ruling applied directly only to state fairs, it presumably will allow limits in other places, such as airports. Those limits, whether on fairgrounds or elsewhere, include confining such solicitors to a booth or similar fixed area.

The ruling leaves the Krishnas and other religious groups free to roam about and speak to whoever will listen. Only when they try to sell literature or seek contributions must they remain confined.

The ruling does not restrict such soliciting on city streets. The ruling made a distinction between practicing "sankirtan" on the street and in an area where "the flow of the crowd and demands of safety are more pressing."

Chief Justice Warren E. Burger and Justices Potter Steward, Lewis F. Powell and William H. Rehnquist joined in White's opinion.

Justices William J. Brennan, Thurgood Marshall, John Paul Stevens and Harry A. Blackmun voted to strike down that portion of the Minnesota law restricting the distribution of free literature.

THE WAY INTERNATIONAL TURNS 40

The Way International will celebrate its 40th anniversary from October 3, 1981 through October 3, 1982. The founder, Victor Paul Wierwille, claims that in 1942 he heard God's call to teach The Word as it had not been known since the first century.

The most significant event of the anniversary will be Wierwille's retirement from the presidency of The Way on October 3, 1982. L. Craig Martindale will be installed as the second president on that date. Martindale was chosen over Wierwille's son, Donald E., now vice president; Howard Allen, secretary-treasurer, and Walter Cummins, assistant to the president. Martindale first took the Power for Abundant Living course class in 1971 and claims to have worked in the past with the Fellowship of Christian Athletes and Campus Crusade for Christ. Since entering the second Way Corps in 1971, he has held more than a half-dozen leadership positions in The Way. Wierwille will maintain control over The Way International as one of the group's three trustees and as the revered "Teacher."

The celebration will offer several special activities to Way followers. Each of the eight regions of The Way of U.S.A. will offer an anniversary weekend, featuring a banquet and a teaching by Wierwille. The Way will also offer a new class, "Living Victoriously," at the New Knoxville Headquarters June 19–July 5, 1982. Open to graduates of PFAL, it is described as "an advanced, advanced class." No fees for the class have yet been published, but they will likely be similar to those demanded at the 1977 filming of PFAL held at Ball State, which netted The Way about $500,000.

SCIENTOLOGY SUED

A lawsuit of $16 million has been entered against the Church of Scientology by Miss Tonja Burden, a former member. She charges that she was made a "personal slave" to the Hubbards, founders of Scientology, while she served aboard the church-owned yacht *Apollo*, and that she was later imprisoned in their Fort Harrison Hotel in downtown Clearwater, Florida.

The church has claimed they do not know the current address of the Hubbards, who are named in the suit. Miss Burden's attorney has asked the federal court to render a default judgment against the church because it appears they have engaged in "a program of planned ignorance" designed to protect the Hubbards from being served with lawsuits and subpoenas.

If the judgment is granted, it will amount to a direct verdict of guilty and leave only the amount of monetary damages to be at issue in the case.

IN DEFENSE OF KRISHNA

On May 15, 1980, California police arrested "His Divine Grace" Srila Hansadutta Swami Maharaja (formerly Hans Kary) for carrying in his illegally imported Mercedes car with false Number plates—a 9mm machine gun, military assault rifles, two loaded pistols and ammunition. Mr. Kary at the time was director of the International Society of Krishna Consciousness for the West Coast, the Pacific and Southeast Asia.

This was only one in a series of discoveries of Krishna arms caches. The Krishnas declare they must be prepared for war and imminent holocaust, and consequently many Krishna children are learning to handle guns.

RAPTURE DELAYED

Bill Maupin of Tuscon, Arizona, and his co-workers in the Lighthouse Gospel Tract Foundation had expected the rapture of the church to occur June 28, 1981. Following a prophetic system similar to that set out in Hal Lindsay's *The Late Great Planet Earth,* in which the date of Israel's becoming an independent nation (May 15, 1948) is used as the starting point for events that will occur within "this generation" (that is, within 40 years), Mr. Maupin expected the rapture to occur on the June date. Figuring that a generation "is exactly 40 years," he dates the second coming as due to occur in 1988 and the rapture 7 years prior to that, namely this year (1981).

Mr. Maupin is still confident the rapture will be before Thanksgiving of this year, but qualifies this by saying that it will not occur until Israel captures Damascus and Lebanon and thus restores its ancient borders. He claims that the Lord showed him that the announced June 28th date with its attendant failure was for the purpose of getting the world's attention so the message of salvation could be presented to them. He is certain that there will be a take-over of the world's economy by the Illuminati as tapes by John Todd have helped him understand. All this should happen very shortly, and he is confident concerning the rapture that "we're going this year."

Pastoral Work

JAMES M. BAIRD
Editor

Jim Baird is the highly innovative pastor of the First Presbyterian Church (PCA) in Macon, Georgia.

Call No Man Teacher, Father, Rabbi . . . or Pastor?[1]

DAVID FOSTER[2]

Down through the years the church has picked up various customs and incorporated them into its life. Some of them are harmless cultural features, peculiar to the society in which the church is located. However, there are other customs which, upon later reflection, have had to be rejected or modified because they contained an unbiblical feature or emphasis. It is easy to engage on an intellectual and theoretical level about the need to change these customs, but it is not easy to effect such changes. This is due to the fact that over the years these customs have become a deeply ingrained part of our everyday life. Consequently, they can only be removed by a thorough and accurate exegesis of God's Word and open, honest preaching mixed with love and patience. The particular custom this article focuses on is the question of whether or not pastors should be addressed by the title "pastor." Let us allow the Bible to speak for itself instead of unthinkingly coasting along with the way tradition has taught us.

Matthew 23:8-10 is the key passage dealing with this issue.

> But you are not to be called "Rabbi," for you have only one Master and you are all brothers. And do not call anyone on earth "father," for you have one Father, and he is in heaven. Nor are you to be called "teacher," for you have one Teacher, the Christ.

The following discussion is on a technical level, not because a simpler discussion based on the English text and English grammar would yield inconclusive results. It is written on a technical level because the people who must first be convinced of this truth are pastors. An argument based on the

---

1. You should find this mildly controversial discussion thought provoking. Responsible replies will be gladly accepted.—ed.

2. Mr. Foster works at Chartwell Baptist Church and at Harbour Rescue Mission in Oakville and Hamilton, Canada.

English text would not set the issue to rest because it might leave a pastor with a lingering doubt. He might think that the finer nuances of the Greek language would throw some different light on the issue.

There are two basic ways of interpreting this passage. Firstly, one may understand Christ to be prohibiting accepting as well as seeking after titles. Here is the question we must try to answer: Is Christ only prohibiting leaders from seeking after titles, or is He also prohibiting them from accepting titles? Is He prohibiting the *whole* practice of calling leaders by titles, or only a *part* of it?

There is some evidence which might be construed to support the more narrow interpretation. (1) Romans 12:11, among other verses, teaches that we are to give honor to whom honor is due. (2) Luke 14:7-11 clearly prohibits seeking honor but equally clearly indicates how fitting it is to honor one who, though not seeking it, still deserves it. (3) Both the preceding and the following contexts emphasize the wrongness of exalting oneself, not the wrongness of being exalted by others. (4) The verb "to call" in verses 8-10 is in the aorist tense, and in particular the ingressive use. A. T. Robertson, an expert Greek grammarian and theologian, argues this ingressive use brings out the sense of *seeking* to be called "rabbi" rather than prohibiting the acceptance of the title when it is spontaneously given (p. 180, *Word Pictures in the New Testament*).

A careful look at the first two above reasons reveals that they are true, but they do not relate directly to this matter of calling a church leader by a title of address. As for point three, there is nothing in the passage which indicates that Christ was restricting His prohibition to the sin of seeking for titles; however, there are clear reasons in the text which show that Christ's prohibition is broader, extending to the overall practice of calling leaders by titles. This second way of interpreting these verses is supported by four reasons.

(1) In these three verses Jesus gave three prohibitions, each with a reason. The three reasons are essentially the same—God is the only true "Rabbi," "Father" and "Teacher." These reasons are fully relevant to prohibiting the practice of calling leaders by titles, but they have less relevance when applied to prohibiting only the self-exalting desire of a leader to be addressed by a title. If I say: "You must not seek to be called 'teacher' because God is the only true 'Teacher,' " you might see *some* logical connection. However, the connection is less than clear. On the other hand, if I say: "You are not to be called 'teacher' because God is the only true Teacher," then you would understand my point clearly.

(2) The above argument is not quite complete and convincing until one looks closely at verse 9. The aorist tense of the verb "to call" is used consistently in verses 8, 9 and 10. If it is meant to convey the idea of seeking, it must do so in all three verses. However, the unmistakable meaning of verse 9 rules out any connotation of seeking. How could this verse have any meaning to the disciples if it has in it the connotation of seeking? Was Jesus saying: "Do not seek to call anyone on earth "father"? Obviously not! The only logical conclusion is that He was prohibiting the practice of calling others by the title "father."[3] If in verse 9 Christ's intent was to prohibit the practice of calling anyone by a title which only God deserves, then why should verses 8 and 10 be saying anything less? Why should the disciples accept the titles "rabbi" and "teacher" when these titles rightfully belong to God? How can Christ be teaching that God is the only true "Rabbi," "Father" and "Teacher" and yet leave the disciples the open option of accepting the titles "teacher" and "rabbi"?

(3) If the above argument has not already convinced you that Robertson's interpretation is weak, then consider these additional points. Robertson's loose paraphrase reads: "Do not seek to be called . . . teacher . . . , if others call you this it will not be your fault" (p. 180, *Word Pictures in the New Testament*). The nuance of seeking which Robertson brings out is not supported by the standard Greek grammars. Blass and Debrunner, for instance, describe the ingressive aorist as denoting "the coming about of conduct which contrasts with prior conduct" (p. 173). Therefore, the idea of seeking for titles, while certainly being included in the scope of Christ's prohibition, is not the only meaning of His words. The aorist simply denotes the fact that something which was being done (by the Pharisees) must not now be started by the disciples). Notice how the NIV translation stays with the simple straightforward meaning. It reads, "You are not to be called 'Teacher' . . . ." The NASB, KJV and RSV also chose to leave out the nuance of seeking.

(4) If Jesus had wanted to limit the prohibition to seeking for titles, He could easily have   (a) chosen other words to express His idea more pre-

---

3. The title "father" was not normally used of leaders. It was a title customarily used in addressing elderly men. See p. 339 in *The Words of Jesus*, by G. Dalman. Also pp. 42, 43 in *The Prayers of Jesus*, by J. Jeremias. Notice how this observation provides a perfect explanation for the change in voice from passive to active. The disciples were prohibited not from being called "father" but were prohibited from calling others (i.e., elderly men) "father." They were, however, prohibited from being called "teacher" because, as men who would soon play key leadership roles in the young church they might soon find themselves being called "teacher," etc.

cisely and   (b) chosen a different reason with which to support His prohibition. If what Jesus wanted to prohibit was only a wrong motive and attitude while still retaining the titles, why did He not choose to use a different reason? Why, for instance, did Christ not use a reason similar to the reasons in Matthew 6:1-4, where He was speaking against wrong attitudes and motives, which, like Matthew 23:1-12, had to do with seeking public honor and attention.

The above four reasons which support the writer's conclusion outweigh the reasons supporting the alternate interpretation. Notice that only one of the opposing evidences has any real validity to it, and this is taken from the near context—one step removed from the immediate context. It is true that both the preceding and following contexts emphasize the wrongness of exalting oneself, not the wrongness of being exalted by others. This single consideration, however, does not have nearly enough weight to overturn the four evidences supporting the writer's conclusion—evidences which, by the way, should be given additional weight because they are all taken from the immediate context (8-10).

Finally, there is one more reason why the broad interpretation should be preferred over the narrow one. The narrow interpretation is consistent with only the one evidence mentioned above, while the broad interpretation is consistent not only with the four evidences used in its support but also with the one evidence used to support the opposing view. The emphasis cited in the preceding and following contexts allows for, but does not point exclusively to, the narrow interpretation. On the other hand, the four evidences which support the broad interpretation exclusively support it. They are not capable of being fitted into the narrow interpretation. In order to uphold the narrow interpretation one must discount and invalidate each of the four evidences. Exegesis of the immediate text and context is always the first and primary task of the interpreter. Only after one grapples with this first step should the correlating passages be seriously examined.

Based on only a discussion of Matthew 23:1-12, there is no other honest conclusion we can come to than the one presented in this paper. A problem arises, however, when we try to correlate other pertinent Scriptures (at least proponents of the other interpretation think so). They think that their interpretation of Matthew 23 fits more naturally with the correlating verses. Specifically, how do they correlate these verses? First, one can observe from even a cursory reading of these verses (I Cor. 12:28; Acts 13:1; James 3:1, etc.) that there are persons in the church who, by way of capacity, function, position or responsibility are "teachers" or "pastor-teachers." They argue this way: "If the Scriptures identify certain persons as teachers, why should it be wrong to address such a person by the title "teacher" as a title of address? The strength of the earlier exegesis seems to give adequate reason for prohibiting the title of address, but for the sake of these who find this unconvincing, we will consider the following. Notice first that the above deduction, which grows out of the other interpretation, has validity, if, and only if, the Bible does not differentiate between a leader having a position or function on the one hand and, on the other hand, having a title of address.

There are many passages which show that the distinction between a title of description and a title of address is biblical. Second John, verse 1, and III John 1 ascribe to John the title of address "elder," but the remaining references to "elder(s)" are merely descriptive of the role or office of elder. It is significant that nowhere in the New Testament (or Old Testament, for that matter) are the terms "rabbi," "father" or "teacher" used as a title of address except in reference to God or Christ. The one and only exception to this is a reference to John the Baptist as "teacher." It is completely understandable that tax gatherers would call him by this title, because to give this kind of title to a widely recognized preacher was the common custom of the day, and Christ had not yet made His prohibition against titles of address. Another observation which seems worthy of note is the fact that there are no New Testament examples of a church leader taking or accepting as a title of address, a title which is ascribed to God. Specific examples of such titles are "Shepherd" (I Pet. 2:25), "Bishop" (I Pet. 2:25), "Apostle" (Heb. 3:1). These above-mentioned observations make it abundantly clear that the Bible does distinguish between titles of address and titles of description. It is, however, quite another thing to locate (or even expect to locate) a correlating verse in the Bible which deals specifically with the appropriateness of titles of address versus titles of description. Having looked at correlative Scriptures and gleaned what is possible, we must admit that there is no strong evidence one way or the other to shed additional light on our interpretation of Matthew 23. The writer sees no alternative but to accept at face value what Matthew 23 says.

Having made a conclusion about what Christ's prohibition means in the text, we now need to explore its meaning for the twentieth-century church. Is it a fair application of these verses to prohibit church leaders from accepting the title "pastor"? One of the reasons that Jesus forbade the use of titles was that they are inconsistent with the equal status which all Christians share. He said, ". . . you are all brothers." This reasoning *seems* to imply that *any* titles, not just certain titles, undermine the basic equality that all Christians share. As we can see from II John 1 and III John 1,[4] this is not quite correct; nevertheless, the remainder of this passage clearly indicates that any title which can properly be ascribed to God is not to be used by anyone in the church. The reason I add "in the church" is that the title "king" is, as far as we can tell, a valid title to use in society, even though God is the only supreme KING. In the context of the immediate family, the title "father" is, of course appropriate for a son to use, and in the king-subject relationship the title "king" is appropriate, but in the community of the church no one is king except God, and no one is the Head except Christ. No Christian has the right to the title "father," even though, like Paul, he may picture himself as the spiritual father of someone by virtue of having led that person to Christ. No Christian has the right to the title "teacher," even though that person may be one of the gifted teachers whom God has given to the church. In the same vein, no Christian has the right to the title "pastor" (literally meaning shepherd), even though he has the responsibility "to shepherd the flock of God" (Acts 20:28). In the Scriptures both God and Christ are referred to as "shepherd," and not merely with a small "s" as in Psalm 23:1, but in numerous instances with a capital "S," denoting his title. The verses in which Christ or God is given the title "Shepherd" are here listed: Psalm 80:1; John 10:11, 14; Hebrews 13:20; I Peter 2:25; and I Peter 5:4. On the basis of these Scriptures there seems to be more warrant for allowing God exclusive rights to the title "Shepherd" (Pastor) than to the title "Teacher." Suppose for a moment that the title "teacher" was not in Matthew 23:10. Would you ever have guessed that, as a title, this innocent term should be reserved strictly for God? Furthermore, how would we be able to establish from the Scriptures that this is a title which belongs only to God? When we come to consider the term "shepherd," we have numerous other Scriptures to guide us in developing and accurately applying the principle contained in Matthew 23:8-10. The conclusion seems inescapable: Church leaders, spe-

---

4. In these verses the apostle John ascribes to himself the title "the elder." Some may wonder whether this contradicts the view presented in this paper. This paper presents an argument against the use of the title "pastor" and any titles which may properly be ascribed to God. "Elder" is not a term which adequately describes God, but the term "pastor" (shepherd) is therefore the title "elder" does not come under the prohibition of Matt. 23:8-10. The title "elder" is found only twice through the New Testament. Leaders are not encouraged to seek to be called "elder," and believers are not instructed to address elders by the title "elder." These facts should caution us against giving leaders a title of address, and in confirmation of this is the significant observation that no New Testament leaders are ever described as having a title of address (other than the above two instances) even though there are frequent occurrences of the terms, apostle and bishop.

cifically those having the position of pastor, should not be called by the title "pastor."

The question naturally arises at this point: If the brotherhood of Christians is inconsistent with some having titles, then is it not also inconsistent to have any distinctions between believers—even the basic distinction between leader and follower? The key to answering this is recognizing the difference between having a position or role of leadership (which is thoroughly biblical) and having a title of address. When one addresses Mr. Smith as "Pastor Smith" or simply as "Pastor," one gives him a title.[5]

Another question arises at this point. Is there not a special sense in which we must give honor to leaders? Yes indeed, there is (notice I Tim. 5:13, 17). It is also important to note that there is one thing that delights a pastor's heart far more than hearing his title. It happens when the believers walk in the truth, thus showing their submissive attitude to the truth which he is teaching them (Heb. 13:7; II John 4).

Now that we have seen what these verses mean and specifically how they apply,[6] you might be wondering: But is there really any difference between a pastor who has only a position and one who has, in addition, a title of address? Does it really make a difference, as long as the pastor doesn't seek the title or get an ego boost out of people calling him by a title? There are four ways in which the difference is evident.

(1) The word "pastor," if used as a title, is used far more frequently in a church than if it is used simply to identify a position. On the practical, though not theoretical, level, this undermines the headship of Christ. On a practical day-to-day basis, the "pastor" is perceived to be the top man (head) of the church. He may not want this and may not even encourage it, but nonetheless it seems to be true in many churches.

(2) The above-mentioned difference in frequency of occurrences of the term "pastor" has another practical consequence. It tends to give the pastor

---

5. It can be quite appropriate to identify Mr. Smith as the pastor, for he does indeed have the position of pastor. I would like to make a suggestion for you to think about. Even though this goes beyond the exact wording of the principle, it is still in harmony with the principle. When speaking of Mr. Smith in a context which does not require that his pastoral position be identified, he should not be referred to as the pastor, for this is essentially the same as giving him the title.

6. There are other areas where this truth might apply, but I do not have the space to explore them here. I would like to encourage you, however, to think about them. What about someone who earns a doctor of theology degree; should he be addressed by the title "doctor"? What about the title "bwana," a colloquial African term meaning "boss," which it has been customary for nationals to use in addressing missionaries? Another difficult question to answer is how this principle applies to the title "doctor" when referring to a medical doctor.

137

added prestige and importance, thus making the leader more of an authority figure rather than a servant leader. While the New Testament does not divest leaders of authority, it does focus on a different kind of authority, an authority which grows out of servant leadership.

(3) Many (perhaps most) evangelical churches believe in the concept of a plurality of leaders which as a group have collective oversight of the church. The deletion of the title "pastor" will help to reinforce and clarify this structure. I believe that this biblical structure is presently clouded and confused in many churches because of the existence of the office of pastor and especially because of the title "pastor." I Timothy 5:17 indicates that the teaching elder is one of the leaders, on a par with them in status, though he is remunerated. It is obvious that I have written this paper with the majority of evangelicals in mind, for my writing assumes that there is an office of pastor distinct from the office of elder. While I do not believe that this distinction is biblical or practical, I do not think it necessary to establish this distinction in order to make my basic point.

(4) Another practical ramification of not using titles is the way it complements the "body life" principle. Ephesians 4:16 and I Corinthians 12 emphasize the importance of the functioning of all the members of the church for healthy growth to occur. Placing undue emphasis on the honor and importance of one member tends to hamper the full and free expression of other gifts in the body. It is generally true that the less significant a person feels he is, the less he will be motivated to become involved. Conversely, the more one member is given special honors unique to him, the easier it is for people to let him do the work. Obviously, there are other factors involved in the dynamic of body life. The fact that a pastor has a title of address is not necessarily the main hindrance to body life functioning, but it can be a significant one.

Each of these above ramifications shows the importance of this principle and should stimulate you to think through the above exegetical arguments again, so that you will come to a firm conclusion. Without a firm conclusion you will not be able to act decisively and effectively.

This brings to mind a whole new area for consideration—how to implement the deletion of the title "pastor." This is no small matter, so it will be necessary to go into it in some depth. There are three basic ways a pastor may respond to this article. First, he may reject the conclusion of this paper and continue to expect his title to be used. Secondly, a pastor may agree with the spirit or essence of the article and yet not make a public announcement clearly declining to accept the title. This approach may be called the middle-of-the-road approach. Because the pastor feels some of the sense of obligation to implement the truth, he may try to do something on a personal level to make individuals feel free to call him by his name rather than his title. The persons to whom he chooses to tell this are those who would not likely be offended by it, i.e., they could adjust to this change fairly easily.

The third way of responding is to make a public announcement to this effect: "I have come to a new understanding of Matthew 23:8-10 (explain it, preferably preach a sermon on it). I realize that it is not going to be easy to adjust to this. There will no doubt be forgetful moments. . . ." This third approach combines patience with courage and love with honesty.

Now, how does one decide which approach to take? First, evaluate whether the prohibition of Matthew 23:8-10 applies to the practice of calling pastors by title. If you decide that it does not apply, then be ready to support your position with solid reasons. Whatever you do, do not hold to your position simply because that is the way you have always interpreted it.

Secondly, evaluate the soundness of the second approach. Those who favor this approach do so for two basic reasons. First, they believe that as long as the title "pastor" is freighted with a minimal amount of honor and prestige, then it does not go against Christ's command (it is simply a title of respect). Two observations argue against this. The reason Christ forbade the titles "rabbi" and "teacher" is equally applicable to the title "pastor," whether it has little or much honor attached to it. As far as Christ was concerned, the key issue was whether or not a title could truly describe what God is. God is my father, my rabbi, my teacher and my shepherd. Only in a secondary sense is any church leader my teacher, rabbi or shepherd; therefore, none of these terms can be ascribed to a man as a title of address. The second reason which militates against the second approach is that it renders Christ's prohibition virtually meaningless. Middle-of-the-road advocates would admit that while the title "pastor" can be so heavily freighted with honor that it would be wrong, it need not always be abused in this way. Pastors can prevent this kind of abuse from happening. Now, if modern day pastors can do this, would it not have been equally possible for the disciples to introduce the title "teacher" with a minimum of honor attached to it? Of course the answer is "yes." If, however, this were the case, why did Christ not couch the prohibition in terms that would allow for this low-profile title? It would seem that there is no other way to take Christ's prohibition than at its face value—it is a clear-cut prohibition against addressing any man with a title that can properly be ascribed to God. Let us not make loopholes in order to perpetuate a tradition which has come into the church long after Christ ascended to heaven.

Let us focus now on a second reason which has been used to support the middle-of-the-road approach. It is felt that this approach gives one the freedom to assent to Christ's prohibition while at the same time avoiding hurting the feelings of those who are very much attacted to the tradition of calling the pastor by title. The main problem with this is that it contains a contradiction. Within the pastor's mind, he renounces any right to be addressed by the title "pastor," but in the meantime most of the church members continue to call him "pastor," and they also probably feel that that is the *proper* way to address him. The contradiction is still present, even though the pastor is, in a modified way, trying to obey Christ's prohibition. If necessary, reread the clear argumentation presented earlier, which shows that Christ was forbidding accepting as well as seeking titles. The pastor should either accept the title as rightfully his, or decline it publicly. Nothing is accomplished by trying to straddle the fence between approaches 1 and 3.

Although the third approach may be correct, those who take it should not underestimate the difficulty and delicacy of their task. We face a longstanding tradition which has become a deeply ingrained habit in many people. It will not be eradicated quickly or easily. It will take tact, courage, time and patience. It will not be any easier to produce instant results in this matter than it is for a sermon on any other deeply ingrained habit (or any sermon, for that matter). Take, for example, a believer who has been negligent or passive in his witness for Christ. It is not likely that he will be suddenly transformed into an active witness after hearing one sermon on the topic. Thorough application of the truth usually takes personal input from someone who cares, someone who can be an example, encourage him and show him how to witness. This third approach which I am advocating is not characterized by sharp rebukes and confrontation so much as by instruction. After all, what we are dealing with is primarily ignorance of a truth, not wilful and stubborn disobedience to a known truth.

A pastor is wise if he first approaches his fellow leaders with the truth that needs to be implemented. After working it through with them, the pastor will be in much better position to share it with the congregation, for he will then have their support. As with the other steps, this one will take time and patience. He will not then be introducing the change all by himself. After the initial instruction on the subject, there might be (will be) the odd time when someone would need to be reminded to forget the title. This reminder could easily be done in a warm, humorous way, and of course it wouldn't be needed every time a person used the title. Often what would probably happen is that a person would catch himself just after addressing the pastor as "pastor." He would likely apologize, but it would not be a cause for embarrassment so much as a cause for others to chuckle with him. Others know just how easy it is to say "pastor" out of force of habit, so they would identify with him and not look down on him.

Suppose that a pastor follows the second approach. He may be able to avoid the delicate and difficult experience of helping tradition-minded people over an obstacle, but he will face another worse predicament. The persons with whom he shares this new-found truth may find themselves being criticized. Word may get around that "he doesn't address the pastor respectfully any more." "I heard him call the pastor by his name, as if he were equal to the pastor." "Has he suddenly become the pastor's special friend, or does he just have a high opinion of himself?" The flexible few whom the pastor hopes will feel free to call him by name will feel anything but free. When surrounded by many who believe in the "proper way" to address the pastor, they will probably feel constrained to continue calling him by his title rather than risk being looked down on by others.

In conclusion, therefore, it is clear that the middle-of-the-road approach does not preserve peace and harmony any more than the third approach. It doesn't seem to help more and more people gradually become free to drop his title. Because of these weaknesses and the above-mentioned exegetical inconsistencies of the second approach, we should forsake it in favor of approach 1 or 3. To choose the first approach (without good reason) is to risk disobeying Christ. To choose the third approach is, at the worst, to risk the temporary negative reaction of some tradition-minded people. Which of these outcomes concerns you most? In the long run, if you follow the third approach, you will retain your position and lose only your title, which is not so important anyway (or is it???).

Preaching

JAY ADAMS
Editor

I Heard It—Did You?

A rare thing happened the other day—I heard a good sermon. Let me briefly analyze it for you, noting some of the factors that made it good.

First, it was *preaching;* it was not a string of stories or a stodgy lecture. By that I mean, from start to finish, the sermon was directed to *us.* We were involved from the outset. The truth of the passage was presented as God's message to *us,* not only to the members of a church long ago and far away in biblical times. God came alive to us as someone living, ruling, caring *now*—for *us.* The preacher made us concerned, and kept us concerned, about *our* families, *our* church, *our* community.

Next, what I heard was *biblical* preaching. What he preached was not an essay on some truth, not the ideas of politicians, media personalities, philosophers, theologians or his own opinions, but what *God* said to us in Paul's letter. Not only did he tell us what the preaching portion means, but he even showed us just how every point that he made comes from the passage. Because he did so, we were able to evaluate for ourselves whether the preacher's conclusions about the text were accurate. Significantly, it was apparent that he had done his homework and that what he told us made sense. And, I believe others in the congregation, if asked, would agree with me that what he said about the text was accurate. He satisfied us that he was preaching what Paul had said. We went away understanding the passage and how everything in the sermon flowed from it. Consequently, we listened to his exhortations about our lives, not as the opinions of a man, but as a word from God to us. He preached, and his preaching was received, with an authority appropriate to the sort of message that it was. We left knowing that we had heard a proclamation from God.

Again, the sermon was *interesting.* The preacher did not cook the juice out of the passage, leaving hard, dry, burned-over abstract teaching. Nor did he serve it to us as a raw, bloody, uncooked chunk of meat. Like a fine chef, he knew just how to handle the passage, cooking it to a turn, garnishing and accenting it so that what he served was the text in full flavor. Its own nutritious juices were preserved, and where delicate nuances otherwise might be missed, he seasoned it with illustrations that brought them out. As he delivered it, the sermon sizzled!

Moreover, the sermon was well *organized*. There were points, sturdy as steel, undergirding the whole, arranged in logical order. But the points did not protrude; he did not bore us with unnecessary firstlies, secondlies and thirdlies, he avoided details that added nothing to the central idea of the message, and—believe it or not—he did not bother us with distracting, forced alliteration. His entire focus in the sermon was on the intent of the Holy Spirit in the text. He kept moving ahead, avoiding all meaningless prefacing and repetition, instead skillfully thrusting each point straight into our hearts!

Now, I know that you will find it difficult to believe me when I tell you that, on top of everything else, that sermon was *practical*. Yes, it really was! It was carefully adapted to the particular congregation to which it was preached. And the preacher persisted in telling us not only *what* to do but *how* to do it. And sometimes, like his Lord in the Sermon on the Mount, he also told us how not to do it. It was plain that he had spent time thinking about what biblical principles mean in everyday living and had worked out biblically derived applications and implementations of each one.

What a sermon it was! You don't hear many like it today. Indeed, because of this fact, you may wonder where it was preached and who preached it. You may ask, ''Are cassette tapes available?'' The answer is no. But I can tell you where I heard it—it was in a reverie while sitting in the Montreal airport that I heard that sermon, and the only record of it is the one that I am now sketching for you *enroute* to Moncton. But, is it doomed to remain merely a bare record, hidden away from the people of God in a pastoral journal sitting on your shelf? Why should it? Why don't you bring it to life? Why don't you preach it this Sunday to *your* congregation? Then, if you and scores of other preachers with you do so, thousands of people throughout the land will truly be able to say, ''I heard a good sermon today!''—J.E.A.

Announcing . . .

A SERMON CONTEST

The *Journal of Pastoral Practice* is conducting a sermon contest. But it will not be like any other sermon contest ever held. Here are the rules:

1. Send a typewritten sermon before September 1982 to the editor of the *J.P.P.*
2. The sermon must be accompanied by
    a. an analysis of the congregation to which it was preached,
    b. a paragraph or two about the purpose and intent of the sermon,
    c. an evaluation of its effectiveness,
    d. an analysis of the sermon in terms of how it was researched and constructed,
    e. and any other significant facts about the sermon.
3. No sermons will be returned.
4. The winning sermon will be published, together with an analysis of it, in a forthcoming edition of the *J.P.P.*
5. If no sermon received is considered worthy of publication, no sermon will be published.

Textual, Topical or Expository Preaching?

"Should preaching be textual, topical or expository?," preachers often ask. The answer to that question is *yes*.

If that answer confuses you, let me explain. How could a good sermon be anything but *all three at once?* The three are certainly not mutually exclusive categories, as some (wrongly) seem to think.

Certainly there will be a text. I prefer to call it a "preaching portion." What must be avoided is isolating a sentence or a fragment of Scripture from its context and preaching from it in that form for one's own use rather than for the purpose for which it was written. Objectionable "textual" preaching neglects telic study and focuses on something in the passage that catches the interest of the preacher. A preaching portion should be determined not by its length (in Proverbs, as elsewhere, one sentence clearly can be a preaching portion), but by whether or not it constitutes a distinctively telic unit. [1]

Certainly there will be a topic. If one has no topic, he has nothing to preach about. What must be avoided is choosing a topic and running from passage to passage to substantiate it, whether the passages do so or not. When a doctrine is taught from two or three passages (that is about maximum), to do so properly requires *extra* effort on the part of the minister. He must study and present textually (in context) each of the passages, doing the exposition that is necessary in all three for the congregation. It is because some preachers do little justice to any passage or group of passages, but merely deliver an essay on a topic, that topical preaching has acquired such a bad press. Good doctrinal preaching (as I prefer to call it) is greatly needed. But it must be textually and expositorally undergirded.

Certainly there will be exposition. By exposition I mean explanation of the preaching portion to the congregation, showing them how he reached the

---

1. A telic unit is a *purpose* unit; i.e., a unit that was designed by the Holy Spirit to effect some particular purpose.

conclusions that he is making in the sermon, thus basing the authority for his exhortations squarely on God's Word (see my other article on preaching in this *Journal*). What must be avoided is mere running comments on a passage that have little or no regard for its *telos* (''purpose'').

As a matter of fact, if all three activities are pursued telically, there will be no problem. It is the neglect of telic analysis and presentation that has led to the various attacks on one or more of these emphases.—J.E.A.